ROUTLEDGE FOCUS

TURNOUT!
Mobilizing Voters in an Emergency

Aimee Allison
Noam Chomsky
Anat Shenker-Osorio
Annie Leonard
Ben Manski
Bill McKibben
Cliff Albright
Dana R. Fisher
Debra Cleaver
Helen Gym
Ian Haney-Lopez
Jeff Merkley
Jennifer Epps-Addison

Maria Teresa Kumar
Winona LaDuke
LaTosha Brown
Lydia Camarillo
Mandela Barnes
Medea Benjamin
Nancy Treviño
Nikki Fortunato Bas
Saru Jayaraman
Stephanie Nakajima
Steve Israel
& others

Edited by:
Charles Derber, Suren Moodliar, and Matt Nelson

Turnout!

Turnout! offers strategies for "emergency elections," like the 2020 race, and spells out the nuts-and-bolts for civic groups and individuals to effectively turn out the vote. Indeed, no election in recent history represents this kind of apocalyptic turning point for our planet and democracy facing profound public health and economic crises. Turnout! is both a creative work of political vision combined with a detailed manual for turning out millions of new voters.

Participation at local, state and federal levels will have an outsized impact on the future of democracy and life itself. The elections also provide an opportunity to power-up social movements that can re-frame and re-define civic participation in an age of extreme inequality, climate change, and pandemics.

Contributors include powerful movement leaders Maria Teresa Kumar (Voto Latino), Aimee Allison (She the People), Winona LaDuke (Honor the Earth), and Matt Nelson (Presente.org); leading public officials advocating greater voter engagement like Oregon Senator Jeff Merkley and Wisconsin Lt. Governor Mandela Barnes, and councilors Helen Gym and Nikki Fortunato Bas. Turnout! reveals strategies and real-world tactics to mobilize millions of discouraged, apathetic, or suppressed voters, including women, low-income, Indigenous, Black, Latinx, Asian, LGBTQIA+, student and youth, and working-class voters.

Charles Derber is Professor of Sociology at Boston College and a noted public intellectual. Professor Derber has written 23 books, including several best-sellers reviewed in the *New York Times*, the *Washington Post*, the *Boston Globe*, and other leading media. His most recent books include *Welcome to the Revolution*, *Moving Beyond Fear*, and *Glorious Causes*. He is a co-editor of the Routledge book series Universalizing Resistance, and is a life-long activist for peace and justice.

Suren Moodliar is editor of the journal *Socialism and Democracy* and coordinator of encuentro5, a movement-building space in downtown Boston. He is a co-author of *A People's Guide to Greater Boston* (2020).

Matt Nelson is Executive Director of Presente.org—the nation's largest online Latinx organizing group, advancing social justice with technology, media, and culture. Matt also served as the organizing director at ColorOfChange.org and has co-founded several cooperative enterprises in multiple Midwestern cities. He was recently featured in the first major book on the Ferguson Uprising, *Ferguson Is America: Roots of Rebellion*. He is finishing a new book on how Latinx organizing and cultural power is reshaping US politics (Routledge, 2020).

Universalizing Resistance Series
Edited by
Charles Derber and Suren Moodliar

The modern social sciences began in the late 19th century when capitalism was establishing itself as the dominant global system. Social science began as a terrifying awakening: that a militarized, globalizing capitalism was creating the greatest revolution in history, penetrating every part of society with the passions of self-interest and profit and breaking down community and the common good. The universalizing of the market promised universal prosperity but delivered an intertwined sociopathic system of money-making, militarism and environmental destruction now threatening the survival of all life itself.

In the 21st century, only a universalized resistance to this now fully universalized matrix of money, militarism and me-firstism can save humanity. History shows that people can join together under nearly impossible odds to create movements against tyranny for the common good. But when the world faces a universalizing system of madness and extinction, it takes new forms of resistance moving beyond the "silo" movements for social justice that have emerged notably in the US in recent decades: single-issue movements separated by issue, race, gender, social class, nation and geography. The story of what universalized movements look like, how they are beginning to be organized, how they "intersect" with each other against the reigning system of power, and how they can grow fast enough to save humanity is the purpose of this series.

The series is publishing works by leading thinkers and activists developing the theory and practice of universalizing resistance. The books are written to engage professors, students, activists and organizers, and citizens who recognize the desperate urgency of a universalizing resistance that can mobilize the general population to build a new global society preserving life with justice.

After Midnight:
How Modern-Day Abolitionism Can Save the Planet
Charles Derber and Suren Moodliar

Revolution Has an Address!
The Transformative Power of Movement Building Spaces
Suren Moodliar

Chomsky for Activists
Noam Chomsky

For more information about this series, please visit: www.routledge.com/Universalizing-Resistance/book-series/RESIST

Turnout!
Mobilizing Voters in an Emergency

Katherine Adam, Cliff Albright, Aimee Allison, Karthik Balasubramanian, Mandela Barnes, Nikki Fortunato Bas, Josh Behrens, Medea Benjamin, LaTosha Brown, Lydia Camarillo, Debra Cleaver, Noam Chomsky, Michael Clingman, Charles Derber, Jennifer Epps-Addison, Dana Fisher, Helen Gym, Ian Haney López, Steve Israel, Saru Jayaraman, Debi Klebansky, Maria Teresa Kumar, Winona LaDuke, Annie Leonard, Bill McKibben, Ben Manski, Jeff Merkley, Kira Moodliar, Suren Moodliar, Stephanie Nakajima, National Elections Turnout Working Group, Matt Nelson, Wilnelia Rivera, Anat Shenker-Osorio, and Nancy Treviño

Edited by
Charles Derber, Suren Moodliar, and Matt Nelson

NEW YORK AND LONDON

First published 2021
by Routledge
52 Vanderbilt Avenue, New York, NY 10017

and by Routledge
2 Park Square, Milton Park, Abingdon, Oxon, OX14 4RN

Routledge is an imprint of the Taylor & Francis Group, an informa business

© 2021 Taylor & Francis

The right of Charles Derber, Suren Moodliar, and Matt Nelson to be identified as the authors of the editorial material, and of the authors for their individual chapters, has been asserted in accordance with sections 77 and 78 of the Copyright, Designs and Patents Act 1988.

All rights reserved. No part of this book may be reprinted or reproduced or utilised in any form or by any electronic, mechanical, or other means, now known or hereafter invented, including photocopying and recording, or in any information storage or retrieval system, without permission in writing from the publishers.

Trademark notice: Product or corporate names may be trademarks or registered trademarks, and are used only for identification and explanation without intent to infringe.

Library of Congress Cataloging-in-Publication Data
A catalog record for this book has been requested

ISBN: 978-0-367-50106-8 (hbk)
ISBN: 978-0-367-50107-5 (pbk)
ISBN: 978-1-003-04882-4 (ebk)

Typeset in Times New Roman
by Apex CoVantage, LLC

Visit the additional chapters: http://emergencyelection.org

Contents

Acknowledgments   xi

PART I
The Emergency Election   1

1 Introducing the Emergency Election   3
CHARLES DERBER, SUREN MOODLIAR,
AND MATT NELSON

2 Our Nation Is Worth Fighting For   10
MARIA TERESA KUMAR

3 To Save Organized Human Society   15
NOAM CHOMSKY

4 Making People Count: The Census and the Vote Matter   17
MANDELA BARNES

PART II
Movements and the Emergency   21

5 Building the Next Progressive Generation   23
AIMEE ALLISON

6 Latinx Social Movements Versus #DeepFakes   29
MATT NELSON AND NANCY TREVIÑO

Contents

7 How We Politicize Our Movements to Build the Country of Our Dreams — 35
JENNIFER EPPS-ADDISON

8 Rocking the Native Vote — 39
WINONA LADUKE

9 The Resistance Is Fueled by Women — 44
DANA R. FISHER

10 It's About the Next Ten Thousand Years — 47
BILL MCKIBBEN

11 The Coronavirus and Economic Crisis: Motivating Voters With Public Goods and Economic Justice — 50
CHARLES DERBER

12 Get Out the Vote for a World Beyond Fossil Fuels — 58
ANNIE LEONARD

13 Your Vote Can Help Move U.S. Foreign Policy From Militarism to Diplomacy — 62
MEDEA BENJAMIN

14 Rebuilding After COVID-19: Equality, Equity, and a Strong Social Safety Net — 69
WILNELIA RIVERA AND KATHERINE ADAM

15 Excite the Vote: It Takes a Community *and a United Front* — 73
CHARLES DERBER

PART III
How We Win — 77

16 Vote Is a Verb: Applying Lessons From Social Science to GOTV — 79
ANAT SHENKER-OSORIO

17	Latino Voter Outreach That Energizes White Voters, Too IAN HANEY LÓPEZ	84
18	Want More Black Voters? Meet Them Where They Live KARTHIK BALASUBRAMANIAN	90
19	Winning Alabama, 2017: A Roadmap to Success? DEBRA CLEAVER	97
20	The Base Versus the Middle: A False Choice STEVE ISRAEL	102
21	Unleashing Our Secret Weapon JEFF MERKLEY	104
22	Voting Ourselves a Raise SARU JAYARAMAN	107
23	Moms for Housing: Inspiring the Movement for Housing as a Human Right NIKKI FORTUNATO BAS	113
24	Public Schools and the Path to a Political Majority HELEN GYM	117
25	Guaranteed Quality, Comprehensive Health Care Coverage From Cradle to Grave STEPHANIE NAKAJIMA	124

PART IV
Turnout! 131

26	How to Turn a Person Into a Voter LATOSHA BROWN AND CLIFF ALBRIGHT	133
27	Eyes South! The Ins and Outs of Voting From Abroad DEBORAH KLEBANSKY AND KIRA MOODLIAR	137

x Contents

28 Voter Assemblies to Protect the Vote — 141
BEN MANSKI AND SUREN MOODLIAR

29 A Letter to U.S. College Students — 152
CONOR L. HICKS, CONNER COLES, JULIANNA
CARBONE, MORGAN JEMTRUD, SOPHIA CARTER,
AUDREY VAS, HANNAH LEBEAU, KARA JOHANSEN, AND
JOHN GEHMAN

Online Chapters (www.emergencyelection.org/chapters)

Red State Rural!
MICHAEL CLINGMAN

Creating Life-long Voters
LYDIA CAMARILLO

Organizing on College Campuses: Working With Bubbles
JOSH BEHRENS

List of Contributors — 163

Acknowledgments

Many more people than even our generous, named contributors made this book possible. They include the many people who are part of their communities. In addition, several friends and allies should be recognized for their generous assistance even though they have not been privy to the entirety of the project and its diverse contributions and are therefore not responsible for its contents. They include Ron Hayduk, Dorotea Manuela, Jason Pramas, Sandra Ruiz-Harris, Paul Shannon, and Victor Wallis. We want to also thank students at Boston College for their help in reaching contributors and their insights in the "Letter to U.S. College Students." They include Conor L. Hicks, Conner Coles, Julianna Carbone, Morgan Jemtrud, Sophia Carter, Audrey Vas, Hannah LeBeau, Kara Johansen, and John Gehman. Dean Birkenkamp and his team at Routledge have been especially kind and generous with their time and advice.

We are, of course, very indebted to our many contributors who put together their pieces quickly and in a rapidly changing world. Each has generously contributed their perspectives even while recognizing that other points of view will likely be published alongside their own. Building on this spirit of generosity, we have not chosen to arbitrate between different pieces and projects. Needless to say, the authors are writing in their personal capacity. Throughout, organizational affiliations listed for identification purposes only.

Part I
The Emergency Election

1 Introducing the Emergency Election

Charles Derber, Suren Moodliar, and Matt Nelson

2020 is the year of an emergency U.S. election. And the decision whether to allow the Trump administration to remain in power will help determine the future of democracy and of life on the planet.

2020 is not the first electoral emergency. The election of Abraham Lincoln in 1860 can be viewed as another emergency election; it led to the Civil War, ended slavery, and helped preserve the nation. So can the 1932 election of Franklin Delano Roosevelt that created a New Deal saving the country from collapse, though Roosevelt would later savage civil liberties by interning 120,000 Japanese Americans. While many elections have significant policy implications, emergency elections have an existential character. The future of the nation and of the planet is at stake.

When Donald J. Trump was first elected in 2016, it was also an emergency election, even if many did not realize it at the time. How much was on the line became clear when millions of people around the world came out to protest during the "Women's March" on January 21, 2017, just one day after Trump's inauguration. In universities, students, faculty, and staff gathered and wept together after getting news of the election results, sharing uncontrollable feelings of grief and fear. The same happened in many workplaces, community centers, and social justice civic and social movement organizations. Communities who were the focus of Trump's hateful rhetoric and threatening promises braced themselves to endure the worst of what the new administration was planning.

After four years of Trumpism, we don't have to guess at the existential dangers. This is a president who sees climate change as a "Chinese hoax" and is trying to shut down regulations that might help reduce toxic emissions and fossil fuel extraction. In fact, he's even banned government officials from using the term "climate change."

Four more years of this, as climate change accelerates without regulatory restraint, spells planetary disaster.

The outbreak of the coronavirus (COVID-19), which President Trump xenophobically refers to as the "China virus," and the massive economic crisis that it triggered, is another reason why 2020 is an emergency election. Never in U.S. history have we seen a public health crisis of this size and danger, which is expected to infect millions of people and kill hundreds of thousands. Nor have we seen an economic crisis of this scale and depth since the Great Depression. The convergence of these two crises affects the wellbeing and very survival of every person in the United States. 2020 is thus an existential election—involving survival of humanity inside and outside the United States because of climate change and the COVID-19 pandemic and economic crisis. And *democracy* is at stake as well, with Trump declaring himself the equivalent of a "war president" with extraordinary powers, and Democrats, at this writing in April 2020, doing little to challenge this or offer their own agenda.

From the Oval Office (or on Twitter), Trump plays the "tough guy" who loves roughing up opponents and dissidents. He is attracted to autocratic leaders of North Korea, Brazil, Russia, India, and Saudi Arabia, and he is eroding the constitutional checks and balances of democracy. Four more years will strain an already weakened U.S. democracy to the limits. At the time of this writing, Trump is feeling exonerated by the failure of the Senate to convict him of impeachment, freeing him to do ever more of the norm-bending, lying, and constitution-breaking that will turn the United States toward unchecked plutocracy and autocracy, which some are calling a "monarchical democracy."

We also know now that many of the Trump administration's wildest promises were not mere rhetoric and demagogy; instead he intended to convert these into policy. From his earliest days in office, he has waged an unremitting war on immigrants and refugees. Turning his attention to cities, he has prosecuted a traditional neoliberal, corporate-friendly agenda with a new boldness to disenfranchise the most vulnerable and people of color, focusing his efforts on the constitutionally mandated census of 2020, and more recently further restricting already miserly welfare provisions. His war of words on Black, Muslim, Latinx, and Asian legislators, coupled with denigrating remarks about African, Caribbean, and Latin American countries, and most recently, a simultaneous embrace of Israel's harshest policies and resuscitation of the ugliest antisemitic tropes, suggest a moral character that is unrestrained by societal norms. Although his racism, in addition to his sexism and homophobia, taps into deep currents, it represents an almost singularly concentrated form of racism, unhampered by those equally deep redemptive forces in American history.

An exceptional character makes for a national emergency—particularly in the COVID-19 era of public health and economic and environmental crisis in which the Trumpist policies will create an even more unequal and oligarchic society. Most of the working population will fall victim to even more ruthless neoliberal, corporate policies that jeopardize everybody, but especially imperil the health and economic wellbeing of millions of working people.

While this is not the first emergency election, it is uniquely important. No election in recent history has been this kind of apocalyptic turning point for the survival of the planet and for preserving democracy in a period of deep public health and economic crisis. It is why we are, during a global pandemic, writing this book. There is no higher urgency, less than a year before the election, than defeating the Trump administration's agenda, the corresponding culture of fear, and the planned spoils of their corporate patrons. Success will require an emergency response, ultimately based on massively turning out people to vote in a nation that has historically had low turnout, partly because elites have worked hard to suppress the votes of those most likely to support a robust social safety net and universal human rights.

We should note that conditions giving rise to the 2020 U.S. emergency election are global, associated with world-wide neoliberalism, global climate change, and the rise of right-wing authoritarian movements around the world, as well as the COVID-19 health emergency and the global economic meltdown that the virus triggered. Emergency elections around the world have led to Trumpist-type regimes in many countries. Trump's 2016 election reflected global trends in health crises and global neoliberalism breeding emergency elections in many nations. While in office, Trump himself bullied countries and intensified global bigotry, nationalism, and authoritarianism. If the Trump agenda persists, it will be a global as well as U.S. catastrophe.

The emergency turnout of enough voters to swing the U.S. election rests on three realities. One is that the country is extremely politically polarized, and it is divided especially closely in "swing states" of the Rust Belt and the Southwest. The country is so polarized that Republican congresspeople tend to dismiss even the threat of COVID-19 as hype and alarmism created to discredit their agenda, compared to Democrats in office who see it as a mortal threat. The second is that because the division is so strong and close in terms of contrasted numbers on both sides of the divide, there are more voters already decided than those easily persuaded. The outcome is thus likely to be determined by who turns out the most voters. The third reality is that there are, nonetheless, important and energized centrist and progressive turnout movements that have already begun and that have an opportunity to swing millions of still persuadable voters as well as to turn out many more millions of historically suppressed and other low-turnout voters.

2020 is within an era in which conservative elites have been able to control the presidency, the Senate, and most state houses after the 2010 sweep into power of the Tea Party. In that fateful year, those in power were able to gerrymander districts, suppress voting, tap billions in corporate dark money after the Supreme Court decision in *Citizens United v. FEC*, and move to intensify the culture wars and gin up hate of Black people, Latinos, women, the poor, LGBTQIA communities, and immigrants, while capitalizing on the Democratic abandonment of the white working class. Reagan Democrats, who were an important part of the emerging Trumpist takeover, helped Republicans fulfill a Southern strategy that linked unlikely bedfellows of evangelical Christians, rural and Midwest white workers, libertarians, and corporate plutocrats into a new Reagan-like revolution that set the stage for the current political epoch that is the primary focus of this book. Reagan's election can be seen as the most recent incipient emergency election, setting the stage for the apocalyptic, full-blown electoral emergency of 2020.

The Reagan revolution led organically to Trump, who would cement the new Republican governing majority into a dominant oligarchy, uniting white workers with their bosses in the name of national glory, white European civilization, and new prosperity for a deregulated, racist, and violent American capitalism. But the capture of the levers of power by Republican legislators should not disguise the progressive attitude on economic issues held by a majority of the U.S. working population. A majority of U.S. adults and voters sees America drowning in a swamp of corruption by billionaires and giant corporations, who are outsourcing workers' jobs, destroying unions, and dismantling social protections created in the New Deal. They see a president prepared to preserve corporate profits over existential threats to public health, the environment, and the wellbeing of the majority of working people in a deep economic crisis.

Progressives can win the 2020 emergency election partly because a majority of the country does not embrace the failed neoliberal economic policies of the super-rich corporate moguls and their political allies—and because the virus and the economic meltdown are making people's economic prospects and health a frightening threat. But it will likely boil down to a very close contest, since millions of whites will vote for the plutocrats because of racism, a feeling of abandonment among ordinary white American working people, and the rage cultivated by callous conservatives against the "moochers" who get welfare and "cut in line." This harmful conservative narrative purports that the moochers are empowered by liberals and socialists, inside and outside of political parties, to get an unfair share of a declining American Dream. Moreover, as the Trump administration slowly acknowledged that the COVID-19 pandemic and its massive economic impact were deadly serious, he has shown the power of the bully pulpit to rally the nation around him to solve one of the worst socio-economic crises ever faced, even though his policies have been inadequate, skewed toward the 1%, and full of bald-faced lies and horrific incompetency and failure.

The bottom line is that voter turnout is key, because the population is closely divided on partisan, geographic, and cultural grounds, and because the United States is historically a low-turnout nation, a democracy based on literally centuries of discouragement or repression of millions of people from voting. Some advanced democratic countries have mandatory voting and get as much as 90% turnout of eligible voters. The United States now tends to get about 60% turnout in presidential elections, and the voters are skewed heavily by race, class, and gender, as well as by constitutional rules that give hugely disproportionate power to people in mainly white states with small populations. Winning elections under these conditions requires emergency level turnout of people, especially in swing states but throughout the nation, who historically have been prevented from voting or discouraged from believing it will make any difference.

How to achieve that turnout is the subject of this short book, which we hope will be read by large numbers of people who realize how desperately important the election is and want to know whether there is anything they can do. The answer is yes! Not only are there things that you can do, but things that you must do to prevent catastrophe. This book lays out as simply as possible the perspectives and nuts and bolts of creating an emergency turnout that can defeat Trump's agenda and shift the balance of power toward a more just, humane, and beloved society.

We have divided the book into several major parts. Notwithstanding their different areas of emphasis, most of the chapters overlap in terms of their subject matter and, in many cases, they could fit easily into any of the parts. Part I, which includes this introduction and three short overviews following it, presents the "big picture" of the emergency election we face and the kind of historical and current emergency turnout that can make a difference.

In Part II, "Movements and the Emergency," civic, political, and activist contributors offer a useful overview of the election in light of particular constituencies and issues. They present their views of 2020 and offer analyses of the political moment. Together, they share the essential context for understanding the 2020 election and show that the anti-Trumpist, democratic opposition has not yet offered a comprehensive, coherent response to the COVID-19 crisis and economic meltdown. Nonetheless, in these chapters, we find the bold alternatives that must be proposed. Needless to say, there are dire consequences if social movements do not gain enough power or fail to champion a response that the public can rally around. Necessarily, this part of the book emphasizes the major political issues—whether public health, the economy and exploitation, climate change, racism, sexism, immigration, human rights, money and politics, and war and peace—all up for grabs in the 2020 elections.

Part III, "How We Win," focuses on both electoral strategy and voting questions. They are vital to who will be allowed to register, vote, and be counted, thus ultimately shaping the outcome of the election. The election specialists who contributed to this section offer insights into how the progressive and centrist coalitions can massively turn out women, people of color, working people, immigrants, and other vulnerable constituencies. This section will also address issues fundamental to building coalitions locally, state-wide, and nationally—housing, jobs, education, and health care, matters all amplified by the COVID-19 pandemic and economic crisis.

Part IV, "Turnout!," focuses on turnout activities and how activists and canvassers relate one-on-one with voters. It has a heavy emphasis on the nuts and bolts, especially as developed by progressive political and social movement organizations with deep experience in elections and turnout. This includes a wide variety of questions, all put in the context of the COVID-19 and the economic crisis—asking and providing answers to how one turns out voters in contexts that make traditional approaches unsafe.

Taken together, the contributions prefigure the broad coalitions of progressives and centrists who will make history in November—either living up to our historical obligations to U.S. history and the global community, or setting the stage for renewed defensive struggles. Although the contributions reveal an underlying and often explicit shared agenda, it is also true that many issues and emphases remain in need of resolution. Politics, by definition, is always incomplete, with the *provisional* "last word" written by people and their movements—even in an election emergency.

2 Our Nation Is Worth Fighting For[1]

Maria Teresa Kumar

On the day right after the presidential election in 2016, at Voto Latino, we went from providing electoral information to suicide prevention information. Soon, our worst fears materialized: we saw a family separation policy and we saw the worst domestic terrorist attack in El Paso since the Oklahoma City bomber. Quoting Trump, the El Paso shooter said that he wanted to stave off the Mexican invasion and stop the Latino voting bloc.

2016 also marked the beginning of a tsunami of young Latinos coming of age that will not crest for another 10 years. Four million young Latinos who heard the president call their loved ones "criminals and rapists" will be eligible to participate in this presidential election for the very first time. Four million. At Voto Latino, we are ready for it.

Translating Across Generations

The idea of bridging generations delineates where we are today in this country. At a personal level, I was translating America for my family long before I turned 18 years old. I was helping them navigate America. I was at the doctor's office helping my grandmother make difficult medical decisions. I was negotiating on behalf of my mother with landlords. And every once in a while, if I must admit, I was also specifically not translating exactly what was happening during parent–teacher conferences, for those who can relate.

But something changed.

For me it was right after September 11, 2001. Like so many young people at the time, the events of the day redefined me. It was time for me to have a real, honest conversation about the path that I wanted to take in this country. I called home that day, back to Sonoma, a small, rural community, to learn that my cousins were not doing so well. One had just been arrested, another had not been able to meet bail, and I realized that at 29 I did not have the words to describe the institutional constructions that had prevented them from accessing a quality education like I had.

So, it was right around September 11 that I redefined where I wanted to go. And I had an honest conversation with myself that while I could've gone into corporate America—I did for a year and a half because I had student loans—what I really wanted to do was to dedicate myself to the Latino community. And to its young people specifically. I recognized that they were leaders in their household long before they were 18 years old; they were making decisions, adult decisions, long before they were 18.

For the next 15 years, that's exactly what I did. Initially, there was no money, just an idea. Despite not knowing what I should do, I decided that Voto Latino was exactly for me because it was the very first organization that said out loud what I deeply felt inside: I was American.

At that point, I was 29 years old. I had gone to the Harvard Kennedy School of Government. I had worked for three years in Congress. I had worked in the state legislature in California. I had done door knocking. But no one had ever said out loud that I was American—even though I fiercely believed that I was. That's what sparked my passion for Voto Latino. I packed my bags, left New York, moved back into my mother's house. She was incredibly generous as it was on the eve of my 30th birthday. The checks that I was writing to her stopped coming, and I funded Voto Latino for the first three years on my credit card.

Fortunately, I recognized that I was in the backyard of Silicon Valley, and the idea behind Voto Latino was that I was going to reach young people on the internet, through culture, through text messaging,[2] and in English—to mobilize them to participate in our democracy. I realized that the reason that there was such inequity in California, and in my hometown of Sonoma, was that people were not participating and people were not asking them to participate.

Responding to Anti-Immigrant Politics

When I was 13 years old, there was a neo-Nazi march in the town next to mine. Confederate flags were flown with impunity. When I was in college, Pete Wilson ascended to the governorship and convinced voters to pass Proposition 187—a "show-me-your-papers" law that targeted my family simply because of their accent and the color of their skin.

No one was safe.

I came home from college that Thanksgiving and convinced my family—my grandmother, my aunt, and my uncle—to become American citizens because we were fearful, concerned, and saddened. That same holiday millions of my peers were having that exact same conversation. Proposition 187 was struck down as unconstitutional, but our community rose, naturalized, registered, and voted, and a state that was a swing state became solidly blue.

It's because I deeply love this country that I do the work that I do. In the last 15 years, Voto Latino has registered over half a million new voters. In the last election, Voto Latino directly registered 15% of all Texas voters, and we deeply believe that Texas is ground zero for our future.

I have had the privilege of spending a lot of time in Texas in the past 10 years. Work at the University of Texas, El Paso. I've seen the transformation of El Paso from a small town into a thriving metropolis that is incredibly generous and incredibly kind, and that is at the crossroads right now of identity of who we are as Americans.

Who We Are as "Americans"

In 2018, within a week of the president's decreeing a family separation policy, we were in Tornillo, Texas, which built the very first camp to intern children—right in the middle of the desert. We brought incredible activists such as Kerry Kennedy, we brought in Dolores Huerta, we brought in MSNBC—they did a three-hour special on the border because we knew that what was happening there was not who we should be as Americans. We built the action not knowing who would come. We had over 500 Americans from across the country jump on a plane, together with a few Canadians, to bear witness to what our government was doing. We knew that it was wrong. What gave us hope, what gave us the opportunity to glimpse the future and to really instill who we are as Americans, was the fact that the people who flew into El Paso and drove to Tornillo, Texas, were American. There were Republicans, there were Independents, and there were Democrats. But what bound us together was the definition of who we were.

This action did not come out of nothing. In fact, right after the presidential elections, when you saw the largest marches of our country's history, what we witnessed was Americans coming together across all states. They were unifying, building on 10 years of marches that bore witness to our country. That past November (2016), 123 million Americans sat out the election; they decided not to vote because they figured that their vote wouldn't matter.

What I mean by "10 years of marches" are the years since 2006 during which the largest marches of our nation's history were led by young Latinos defending the rights of their parents. Over two million people took to the streets in 2006. Shortly after, we saw Occupy Wall Street. Young people there were calling out the disparities in our country that no one was paying attention to. We saw climate change marches; we saw marches when it came to this idea that we had to have equality and fairness when it came to marriage. You saw Black Lives Matter protesters come out, and we saw Americans come out for the Women's March, which Voto Latino helped coordinate across the country in all states. But I thought what was beautiful was that it was in the red states that Americans say we are going to bear witness.

A New Intersectional, Generational Politics

One of the hardest things that we witnessed at Voto Latino after Election day was the sudden realization that Deferrred Action for Childhood Arrivals was threatened. The Dreamers had given their information to the federal government, now headed by Trump, which basically said that it was going to track down the Dreamers.

We worked with our college chapters. From Oregon all the way to Pennsylvania, every single college Voto Latino chapter president had experienced a racial incident. We could have retreated but at the end I said well "what would you guys like to do?"

And the young people said, "We want to have cross-cultural conversations, intersectional conversations. We want to talk to college presidents. We want to talk about the issues that we care about. Will Voto Latino help us?" We started coordinating young people so that we went from 9 college chapters to over 28 college chapters, and by the end of next year we are going to have close to 32 city chapters. But in order to have a college chapter on your campus, you have to pledge that you are going to start with an intersectional conversation bringing in diverse groups and diverse conversations, because that is what we need right now. There is plenty of divisiveness, telling us who is American and who is not. But when we have conversations, when we bring people in, when we encourage people to have those tough talks, we're stronger for it.

In the last election, millennials and baby boomers made up roughly 62 million people on both ends of the population spectrum. This coming election, we're going to have roughly 12 million more young people than baby boomers. What gives me hope is that the 2018 election was the biggest participation in a midterm election in close to a hundred years. What did that tell me? That our elections matter, that people all of a sudden realized that in our democracy, in order for it to be robust, in order for it to be strong, we have to love it, we have to care for it, we have to tend to it.

One out of six voters this past election were young voters, and what did we see the next day? We saw people going from resisting to occupying our institutions, and I deeply believe that the institutions reflect the country they serve, those people who vote.

There are so many more people, so many more Americans who share our values and vote our values. This past election (2018), we saw over 126 women go into Congress for the very first time. In our country's more than 240-year history, this Congress is the most diverse that we've ever seen. We often hear the most progressive voices, but when you look at the map of the people who entered Congress, they are reflective of our values. They're individuals who deeply believe that in order to fix America, you must roll up your sleeves and get into it.

Notes

1. This is a revised and condensed version of a speech by Maria Teresa Kumar. The Original Speech May Be Viewed Here: "2019 Posey Leadership Award—Maria Teresa Kumar—GO! Forum at Austin College." Accessed March 27, 2020. www.youtube.com/watch?v=ZOvFKBHZFWA.
2. Tim Grieves. "Rgm Chng Bgns @ Hm: A Drive to Register Voters via Text Messages." *Salon*, August 24, 2006. www.salon.com/2006/08/23/text/.

3 To Save Organized Human Society[1]

Noam Chomsky

It was not in doubt that 2020 would be a fateful year, especially so for those who care enough about the world to try to determine its fate—for activists, in brief.

One reason is that 2020 brings us an election in the most powerful state in world history. Its outcome will have a major impact not only on the United States, but thanks to U.S. power, on the perils faced by the entire world.

The nature and scale of these perils were underscored at the year's outset when the hands of the famous Doomsday Clock were set, providing as good a succinct assessment as we have of the state of the world. Since Donald Trump's election, the minute hand has been moved steadily toward midnight, meaning "it's over." As 2020 opened, the analysts abandoned minutes and turned to seconds: 100 seconds to midnight, the closest to terminal disaster since the first setting of the clock in the wake of the atom bomb attacks. The reasons were the usual ones: the severe and increasing threat of nuclear war and of environmental catastrophe, with the White House proudly in the lead in racing to the abyss; and the deterioration of functioning democracy, the one hope for dealing with impending disaster.

There is time to save organized human society (and many other species) from cataclysm, but not much. How much depends in no small measure on the U.S. election in November 2020, which may turn out to be the most important election in human history, perhaps coming close to sealing the fate of organized human society.

Extreme words, but are they an exaggeration? Four more years of Trumpism might raise global warming to irreversible tipping points. At the very least it would sharply raise the costs of assuring some measure of decent survival. Trump's dismantling of the thin barriers to nuclear destruction might well succeed in setting off a final war; and even if not, will drive the world closer to the brink. Another term will also provide Mitch McConnell with more time to pursue his assault on democracy by cramming the judiciary with enough young far-right justices to ensure that deeply reactionary and destructive policies will persist no matter what the public would prefer. For these reasons alone—there are many others—every effort must be expended to prevent this tragedy; and if it occurs, to redouble efforts to limit the damage and open the way to a livable world.

Note

1. This is an excerpt from the forthcoming book, Noam Chomsky, Charles Derber, Suren Moodliar, and Paul Shannon. *Chomsky for Activists: Universalizing Resistance*. London and New York: Routledge, 2020.

4 Making People Count
The Census and the Vote Matter[1]

Mandela Barnes

It was just a year ago when I was sworn in as Wisconsin's first Black lieutenant governor, where I could represent those in our state who feel they may have not been represented before; to be in a position where I can be a voice for those in our state who have felt voiceless; to be in a position where I could work to create and support policies that allow everyone in our state the opportunity to thrive.

I take pride in the work we're doing at the State Capitol to build a more equitable and just society, and I strive to continue that work for everyone.

Many of us, including myself, dream of a day when everyone in our state, including our Latinx communities, can have equitable access to quality health care, good schools, and a clean environment—but it means nothing without putting in the work to get it done.

That's why I'm fighting to bring equity to our neighborhoods that suffer disproportionately from the effects of climate change through my work on the Governor's Task Force on Climate Change.

That's why we support giving undocumented immigrants access to driver's licenses. Doing so will make our roads safer and eliminate the fear of working mothers and fathers being separated from their children.

We also support providing undocumented students in Wisconsin with in-state tuition, so they can have access to quality, affordable education and can have the opportunity to build a strong future for themselves and their families.

We must work together to usher in a new chapter where all people are treated with dignity, can provide for their families, and can pursue their dreams.

Voting Rights

As we continue to work toward justice and equity at the State Capitol, I challenge each of you to do your part in your communities by being civically engaged. With that said, we need to make sure people don't lose their voting rights.

Right here in Wisconsin, there is a court battle going on now over whether to remove voter registrations of more than 200,000 people.[2]

In recent years, those in power in Wisconsin have worked diligently to disenfranchise the vote of our communities of color—from gerrymandering our districts to making the simple task of voting unnecessarily difficult.

Wisconsin is by no means unique or unusual. All across our nation there are concerted efforts by some elected officials and legislative bodies to silence Black voices and the voices of our communities.

I have a responsibility as Lieutenant Governor to make sure that opportunity exists in every part of Wisconsin for every resident. Our governor and I understand that this includes ensuring that everyone in our state has a voice and a vote.

We need to maintain people's access to the ballot. Our community's voices need to be heard and need to count.

Census

A part of that is being counted. I cannot stress enough the importance of this year for multiple reasons. Most importantly, being counted in our census.

Our census takes into account location, race, education, income level, and many other factors that determine where and how our resources should be distributed.

Unfortunately, there are systematic disparities in how our system takes into account everyone, and they include the factors I just named.

Our governor created a Complete Count Committee for the 2020 census, which will work to increase outreach and participation in the upcoming 2020 census, particularly among populations who are at risk of being undercounted.

Kids ages five and younger are less likely to be counted. People of color, along with people with lower incomes and lower levels of education, are also less likely to be counted.

In a state that deals with both the legacy of and present-day racism, along with disparities between our rural and urban communities, we must take all the steps necessary to ensure everyone has a voice.

Simply put, our government can't account for those we don't know exist.

Closing Words

I believe in the power of inclusion, the power of strength, and the power of unity. But we also must remember that unity is journey, not a destination.

A journey to recognize that all of us have more similarities than differences. A journey to come together and see that each of us have equitable opportunities for success.

During this journey, we must fight with vigor to address all the inequities that divide us. We must make our state and our country a place where everyone has the opportunity to thrive.

Notes

1. While addressing the practical matters associated with the COVID-19 emergency, Lt. Governor Mandela Barnes shared this lightly edited transcript of a recent speech to emphasize the close connection between the census, the battle to protect voting rights, and the substantive issues of the day, including immigrants' rights, extreme inequality, and climate change.
2. Timothy Zignego v. Wisconsin Elections Commission, No. 2019AP2397, 2020AP112 (Court of Appeals, State of Wisconsin February 28, 2020).

Part II
Movements and the Emergency

5 Building the Next Progressive Generation

Aimee Allison

Three to 5 percent. This is what we need in 2020. If the turnout of women-of-color voters increases by 3 to 5 percent from our numbers in 2016, we can win the White House, secure the House of Representatives, and win the Senate majority. This is how important the votes of women of color are.

We're in trouble in this country. Under the leadership of President Trump, the far-right is dismantling the fabric of our political and civil society, through repeals of laws safeguarding civil and human rights, education, immigration, and the environment. But all is not lost. The very people who have been ignored, taken for granted, discounted, and dehumanized are the ones who are going to save us. I'm talking about the saving graces of our democracy. I'm talking about women of color.

Women of color are running for office in record numbers. We are the fastest growing voting bloc, the bedrock of progressives and centrists, and we are now poised to make substantive changes to the makeup of our political institutions. We are among the best political minds of this (and any) generation, and we have already changed the game in American politics.

Here's the thing: from the beginning of this election cycle (and my entire life really), we've heard that we need to win "moderate" white voters to win. We are told that we need conservatives, too. This message has been a drumbeat of establishment Democrats, even as the demographics of the country are transforming—we are now 38% people of color overall, and in many states people of color are the majority. Appreciating this demographic reality means we need to work with a *new* calculus, one based on *new* political facts. The key to securing a progressive future for our country is the New American Majority, the multi-racial coalition of voters that elected Barack Obama. We are growing fast and are the most progressive voters.

We are also the most reliable Democrats. It's been tough work to convince political strategists, donors, and party leaders to change their assumptions and biases about what it takes to win elections. It was and continues to be difficult to get resources for voter engagement and voter turnout in communities of color.

The 2016 election should have taught the Democrats that their old playbook wasn't working. Old notions about whose vote and voice matters in elections—wherein 75% of the Democrats' billion-dollar war chest was spent on white moderate and conservative voters—did not result in a White House win. In the business of electoral politics, how such immense financial resources are spent translates into choices about who gets a call, what words are used to attract voters, who is in the commercials, which candidate gets support, how policies are framed, and which communities are shown political love. Money produces the flurry of political consultants calling plays, donors making bets, and analysts conjuring trends. Think about this: the Hillary Clinton campaign spent next to nothing on Black voters until just six weeks before her 2016 election. This hubris and resulting ineptitude shaped how the Democratic Party as a whole campaigned in 2016 and continues to campaign in 2020. It is reflected in how moneyed interests like Emily's List spend millions to woo a shrinking slice of the Democratic Party voters (i.e., white voters, mostly moderate and conservative), while largely ignoring the rest. It resulted in ignoring the New American Majority, who represent half of the Democratic voters across the country.

So we know what happened in 2016. Inconceivably, the election was decided in the Electoral College in battleground states in the Midwest, the South, and the Southwest, and the Democrats lost both houses of Congress. One statistic says it all: 85% of married white women voted for Trump, 53% of all white women. The Republican agenda won. And the rest of America lost.

That was 2016. We have another bite at the apple in 2020.

Now is when the new story begins. Out of the disarray and obsolescence of old Democratic Party practices, new and beautiful possibilities are emerging. Right now in swing states like Arizona, Florida, Texas, Georgia, Michigan, and Alabama—places that President Trump won—women of color are leading the charge by engaging new and young voters and people of color. We understand that our swing voters are not the ones moving from red to blue. The swing is from nonvoters to voters. Right now, Latina, Asian American, Native American, and Arab American women are leading efforts in battleground states. Women of color are claiming space in blue districts

Building the Next Progressive Generation 25

where tired moderate Democrats don't fight for us, challenging the GOP in places like California where the majority of women are Black and brown and the majority of voters are women.

In the battleground states of Arizona, Florida, Georgia, Michigan, Pennsylvania, Texas, and Wisconsin, the number of women of color who voted in 2012 to reelect President Barack Obama was greater than the number that did not vote in 2016. In several of these states, there was a lower women-of-color turnout in 2016 than in 2012. There is a great opportunity to flip these swing states from red to blue in 2020 *if* we motivate and inspire women of color to vote. The numbers show our power. *A 3-to-5% increase in women-of-color turnout in battleground states will capture enough Electoral College votes to win the White House.* What's more, in several of these states, women of color could deliver Senate seats and the Democratic majority—Arizona, Georgia, Texas, and Alabama, to name a few.

The only path for a winning progressive agenda is paved by the enthusiastic and concerted support of women of color. We women of color will lead an inclusive, multi-racial coalition to victory in the primaries and 2020. First, women of color are six times more likely to vote for a Democrat than white men are. Among Democrats, women of color make the difference in primaries. In the 2020 Democratic primary, women of color were the most influential voting block: women of color are 47% of Alabama's Democrats, 31% of California's, and 33% of Texas's. In Virginia, the state that secured a Democratic majority in both state houses in 2019, women of color are 21% of Democrats. Any candidate aiming to win a Senate seat or the presidency would be foolish to ignore women of color as a powerful electoral base and as policy leaders. Research from the data firm Catalist shows that women of color have the strongest propensity to cast Democratic votes, and 88% supported Democrats in the 2018 midterms, compared with 48% of white women and 38% of white men (Figure 5.1).[1]

Who wins the White House will be determined by who focuses squarely on the Sun Belt (the South and Southwest). Imagine if a year ago the political parties invested hundreds of millions to turn out our Black and brown voters. The greatest opportunity to win a progressive future for generations to come is to invest deeply in voters who are eligible to vote. This investment wouldn't be focused on election day; they would build staff, organizations, tools, relationships, and lists year round. Research shows, and women of color prove, that the best voter turnout approach is person to person from a trusted friend, family, or neighbor.

26 *Aimee Allison*

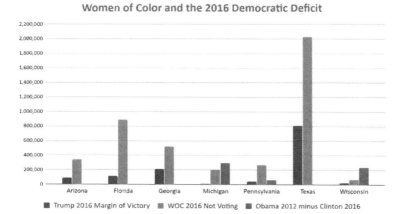

Figure 5.1 Women of color have the strongest propensity to cast Democratic votes.

More new information: Women of color are one in four voters in key swing states. Women of color make up more than a quarter of all Democrats. Looking at recent history in the 2018 midterm elections, women of color were crucial to Democrats' 2018 victories.[2] Turnout among women of color increased 37% compared with the 2014 midterms. Asian American and Pacific Islander women increased 48%, Black women 28%, and Latinas 51%

Finally, over the last decade, when turnout among women of color has been above the national average, Democrats have won. When their turnout is below, Democrats have lost. Clearly parties will do well to win over women of color.

Now that I've made an argument about how critical the women-of-color vote is, some might adopt the view that women of color can save the country. Women of color *can* do the critical work of turnout, and deliver votes. *But* successful turnout efforts need to go further. It is not enough for Democrats to say to women of color "vote blue no matter who." Successful turnout will follow the lead of women of color *and* focus on issues that move women of color (our poll in Nevada showed that health care and racism topped the list).

I founded She the People to build the political power of women of color and to tell the new story to the nation, to build our collective political power, and to lead the country forward. She the People upholds four fundamental values: to love our own and others, to seek justice for all, to ensure that everyone belongs, and to make sure that our democracy lives up to its greatest promise.

Women of color want to build power, not just win an election.

Women of color are leading a multi-racial democratic coalition that will win in swing states and beyond. And these victories are not about electing Democrats. We women of color have bigger plans for the nation. We're seeking economic and racial justice. We want a country where people can live lives of dignity. This means full access to health care, housing, and education. This means living in the democracy that we've dreamed of but have not yet realized. It's a politics we have not yet seen.

We know this can be done because it has been done. Look no further than Stacey Abrams's gubernatorial race in 2018. Her campaign was different from any previous statewide effort in Georgia. From its beginning the strategy, resources, and focus were built on maximizing turnout of people of color: recognizing and expanding the power of Black women who were nearly 40% of Democratic voters, *and* building powerful relationships with voters in the Latinx and Asian American communities. This was a long-term play, not one relying on either a last-minute ask or an assumption of support.

Her campaign had legions of organizers knocking doors in suburban, rural, and urban areas for a year and a half. Her staff reflected the diversity of the state, and they brought cultural know-how into every aspect of the effort. They invested in bilingual canvassers, volunteer cards with seven languages, and urban and country radio. This was not a run-of-the-mill effort of a politician attempting to win a Southern state, with a heavy reliance on TV and digital ads.

And through this strategy, Abrams changed the political landscape in Georgia. In 2014, 1.1 million Democrats voted. In her election, 1.2 million Black voters cast their ballots for her. Her approach tripled Latinx and Asian Pacific Islander voting rates. And in a state where the Democrat consistently loses the white vote, she increased her share of that electorate to levels that matched Bill Clinton's. In all, her campaign turned out a record 1.9 million voters, including 800,000 who previously didn't consider voting in a midterm election. Officially she lost by 55,000 votes in the face of egregious voter suppression and purges at the behest of the Georgia Secretary of State, who was also her opponent, Brian Kemp. Eventually, he claimed the seat, laying bare the democracy-destroying practices that muzzle communities of color and were made "legal" by the right-wing state legislature. But the electoral stage for 2020 is set to be competitive from city council to the state house to the presidency itself.

And Abrams's race laid bare the real danger of vote suppression and the need to couple turnout efforts with robust multi-state, coordinated efforts to protect the vote.

Stacey Abrams knew what is needed for states in the South and the Southwest, in the Midwest and beyond: that the New American Majority, led by women of color, is the keystone to victory. In Georgia, top leaders such as New Georgia Project's Executive Director Nse Ufot listened to voters, built relationships, held events, registered voters, checked registration, and led door-to-door efforts. In Florida, Arizona, Texas, and other states, now there are talented women of color running year-round efforts to expand the electorate. When determining who to support and invest in, look at the organizations that are grounded in a year-round effort to expand the participation of people of color. These are the efforts that matter most in turnout. These are the organizations that will be in the community after the election is over. Learn from and support the leaders crafting this new multi-racial democratic coalition, building infrastructure and engagement, including Andrea Mercado in Florida, DeJuana Thompson in Alabama, Tram Nguyen in Virginia, Michelle Tremillo in Texas, Stephanie Cho in Georgia, Latosha Brown in Georgia, and Montserrat Arredondo in Arizona.

There are so many more.

She the People is about our faith in a politics we have not yet seen. We want a country where people can live lives of dignity. And we will insist that whomever receives our votes and our support will govern with our deepest values and full humanity in view.

Women of color are the saving graces of our democracy. We are holding up moral standards for the rest of the nation. We do this not only for women of color. We do this for all of us in America.

Shoulders back, hearts open, we're together in this.

Notes

1. "CATALIST-What Happened Last Tuesday: Part 2—Who Did They Vote for?" Accessed March 17, 2020. https://docs.google.com/spreadsheets/u/0/d/1kpkG3Ll2V7YZrnBCpUqbfsXWXOisVY556hb_LUO2ncI.
2. Bonnie Chiu. "The Spike in Political Mobilization of Women of Color in the U.S. Will Define 2020." *Forbes*, September 18, 2019. www.forbes.com/sites/bonniechiu/2019/09/18/the-spike-in-political-mobilization-of-women-of-color-in-the-us-will-define-2020/?fbclid=IwAR2ONuWGCn2np8lA5dBU1kV9UinRTNqaU8vzu-DcsD_Go_U5d4y4o8xoW0o#10e6e048367f.

6 Latinx Social Movements Versus #Deepfakes

Matt Nelson and Nancy Treviño

It's personal. Our country has been enduring a flood of hateful, White-supremacist attacks combined with brutal (and often deadly) federal policies. The effectiveness in meeting this moment depends on the ability of activists and organizers to build strong social movements, while continuing to raise up new generations of leaders. Movement-building also requires millions of people who are inspired to take consistent action and make deep investments in creating a new political imagination, one that transforms the culture and politics of our nation.

Suitably, Latinx people are on the frontlines of social movements. An election year, especially one with such high stakes—during the health and economic crisis sparked by COVID-19—underscores the need to exercise the power of social movements to protect the most vulnerable and to win elections nationwide. With the pandemic hitting our nation and deeply impacting our economy, the Latinx community is especially vulnerable due to our income levels, migration status, workforce representation, and high levels of small business entrepreneurship. Our social movements will have to create and organize around progressive policies at a mass scale that is strong enough to shape candidates, realize political power at the polls, normalize effective digital organizing, and combat disinformation to protect the integrity of the 2020 election.

Diverse, dynamic communities are building a new transformative politics that is very interpersonal, community-oriented, transracial, transnational, and powerful despite a lack of heavy financial resources—or investments—in these communities. Latinx people, when we are at our best, advance an intersectional, multi-racial agenda that does not leave behind communities that are often left behind, such as Black, LGBTQIA, and Indigenous Latinx communities. And in 2020, the spotlight is turning to Latinx voters, particularly younger and first-time voters, who had an incredible impact on the primaries and may tip the balance of power in the general election.

So, what does a progressive "Latinized," pro-democracy movement look like? The promise of the United States is democracy—a system of government in which the people hold the ruling power. And Latinx communities, at 60 million strong, are poised to attain greater political power and shape the United States in ways that can turn that promise into reality producing a bold transformation. In addition to our sheer numbers, we are a *young* population—half of Latinxs are not old enough to vote, with around 900,000 of us turning 18 each year.[1] Latinxs are creative and resilient people, who are leaders in households, communities, and all sectors of the U.S. culture and economy.

Over the years, Presente.org, the nation's largest digital Latinx organizing group, has spoken to thousands of Latinx canvassers, organizers, and political leaders. Besides asking a registered voter to vote, it is important to engage every single person in a household and to follow up even in non-election years. But first we must lay the groundwork and use our cultural strengths—and digital organizing power—to get there. During this hyper-political and more online-focused era, more people are tapping into "activist knowledge" while creating authentic and personal relationships with voters, both online and offline, and letting them know that a given organizer (or candidate, or political party) has their backs.

The overall youthfulness of U.S. Latinx people—the youngest of all U.S. demographic groups—means that once you earn our trust, you've got a loyal voter or supporter of your cause for decades to come. With a median age of 28, Latinxs are the nation's youngest population.[2] For context, the median age for White Americans is 43, followed by 36 for Asian Americans, and 34 for African Americans. The demographic shift alone does not determine our destiny. Voter outreach needs to be accompanied by more hands-on engagement with Latinx voters. Some of the electoral lessons of 2016 and 2018 hold the key to translating our growing numbers into greater political power.

The 2020 emergency election will be a huge test of our social movements. Historically, our movements have not fully integrated voter engagement into our day-to-day organizing work and we can no longer afford to do this.[3] More than $10 billion will be spent by presidential candidates as they fight their way to the White House. Political ads are plastered across the internet, not to mention the deluge of ads on television and radio.[4] U.S. voters will have to decide which candidates best align with their values while facing massive disinformation efforts aimed at swaying their votes. Pro-democracy Latinx social movements will have to battle big money in politics by providing bold demands and powerful organizing to drive voter turnout and ensure presidential candidates address the issues most important to their bases. The movements' futures depend on the outcome of the 2020 election, and it's up to us to take audacious action.

As candidates run campaigns to persuade the U.S. electorate, it will be imperative for social movements to shape policy priorities and win elections. Latinx voters must be mobilized to vote in huge numbers during these trying times. Our social movements need to ensure our voices are included and empowered in candidates' agendas. These must affirm human rights-based public health, civil rights, and economic justice solutions for Latinxs and all working-class people in the United States. In the contested primaries, 2020 presidential candidates adopted policies shaped by frontline communities—including bans on private prisons, calls for universal health care, expansion of affordable housing, and pathways to citizenship for the 11 million undocumented people across the U.S. This demonstrates the influence social movements can have on elections. This is due to the powerful grassroots organizing—online and offline—led by communities of color.

Social movement academics, like Manuel Pastor and Rhonda Ortiz, have identified the key elements necessary for strong and durable social movements.[5] They argue that our movements require a vision and substantial membership bases with a deep commitment to fighting for the long haul. We must also have a vision for governance, research to elevate our bases' personal stories (necessary to shift narratives), and clear policies to achieve systemic change. We also need to scale up organizations, have a strategy for scaling up, and have a plan for building power among various movements for broad social change. And, most importantly, we must have a plan to *turnout voters on a massive scale.*

Since 2016, social movements have shifted strategies in the field, resulting in historic voter turnout during the 2018 midterm election. Organizers instituted relational organizing programs coupled with deep canvassing to reach large voter bases. These tactics drove Latinx people to hit the polls during early voting and attend rallies in support of their preferred candidate.[6] Our movements were instrumental in electing a new wave of progressive candidates like Alexandra Ocasio-Cortez, who is part of an inspiring "squad" of women of color championing reproductive rights and the Green New Deal.[7]

The 2020 emergency election brings us to two key elements that will dictate the future of our democracy: disinformation and the power of digital organizing. Massive amounts of disinformation, or strategic-distortion campaigns, have spread across social media since the 2016 election, reaching millions. Facebook and Twitter have played a major role in allowing disinformation to infect the American psyche, a role that continues today. Disinformation will once again have a stark effect on voter turnout during this election, and it will take powerful digital organizing to battle these untruths.

As we are writing this, our country and the planet is experiencing the COVID-19 pandemic. It is yet another challenge that will affect voter turnout, and we will need to get creative as we work our digital organizing muscles. We are already organizing digital mass actions, meeting virtually, and campaigning online to get out the vote. It's up to us—especially those of us who are already executing exceptional digital organizing campaigns—to do everything that we can do to help groups power up their digital organizing. Meeting this moment for lead organizations requires adopting new language and new forms of outreach, filling communications gaps, supporting strategy, and adding to the communications and mobilizing capacity for frontline communities.

Disinformation tactics are becoming more sophisticated, with Trump's re-election campaign being at the forefront of these divisive efforts. The campaign plans to spend $1 billion to send out troves of bots, micro-targeted ads, and mass text messages to foment fear in voters across the country.[8] These insidious channels seek to fracture our burgeoning movements, but if we successfully create digital infrastructure to combat disinformation, direct our collective power with masses of boots on the ground, and strengthen our alliances, we will help ensure the integrity of the vote. And as Samuel Woolley adds, "we must build technological detection and mitigation systems with ethics at the forefront."[9] Leading Black activists have already taken concrete steps to address disinformation tactics by creating both a system to help activists flag suspicious accounts and a digital security team who will investigate.[10] Furthermore, political campaigns have committed to steer away from unethical digital tactics that would further undermine the integrity of the 2020 election.[11]

Building robust social movements led by Latinx people can have a transformative effect on the country's next four years. It will take solid organizing and alliance-building to push candidates to support the policies created by our communities. California, Texas, New Mexico, Florida, New York, and Arizona have the highest concentration

Latinx Social Movements Versus #DeepFakes 33

of Latinx voters and are where we should concentrate our efforts.[12] Additionally, Nevada's Latinx population makes up almost 20% of the state's registered voters and can play a decisive role in how our communities flex their political power.[13] Arizona has already seen the impact of the Latinx electorate, with Kyrsten Sinema flipping a U.S. Senate seat in 2018 thanks to 70% of the Latinx vote.[14] Further concentrating Latinx voter power will continue to transform Arizona's political future, with yet another contested Senate seat up for grabs in the 2020 cycle.

Despite the tremendous Congressional victories during the 2018 midterm elections, some organizations targeting Latinx voters didn't plan and execute electoral programs efficiently. The Latino Vote Project identified missed opportunities that we can implement to ensure that our values of dignity and human rights wins this emergency election.[15] We have a lot to lose if the current administration's agenda remains in the White House for four more years—the catastrophic effects of climate change will be ignored, the Department of Homeland Security will ramp up deportations, income inequality will be exacerbated, and millions will continue to live without health care.

Every opportunity should be seized to contest for power. 2020 is the year of an emergency U.S. election. Whom we elect will help determine the future of democracy and of life on the planet. Latinxs comprise one fifth of the U.S. population. By 2060, almost one third of the U.S. population is expected to be Latinxs. The interests of humanity as a whole correspond with the interests of the Latinx people to the extent that Latinxs are Black, brown, white, transnational or immigrant, Indigenous, multi-faith, feminist, LGBTQIA, poor, and working class. Latinx identity, therefore, has the power to embrace all of its intersectionality in a way that corresponds with the unity of, and solidarity with, oppressed, colonized, and exploited people around the world.

Notes

1. Natalie Montelongo. "Latinos and the Fight for Voting Rights." *Forbes*, November 16, 2017. www.forbes.com/sites/civicnation/2017/11/16/latinos-and-the-fight-for-voting-rights/.
2. Antonio Flores. "How the U.S. Hispanic Population Is Changing." *Pew Research Center*, September 18, 2017. www.pewresearch.org/fact-tank/2017/09/18/how-the-u-s-hispanic-population-is-changing/.
3. Billy Shore. "Stop Sitting on the Sidelines, Nonprofits, and Get Out the Vote." *The Chronicle of Philanthropy*, September 12, 2018. www.philanthropy.com/article/Opinion-Getting-Out-the-Vote/244487.

4. Laura Castro Lindarte. "Nearly $10 Billion Will Be Spent on Political Ads in 2020." *Roll Call*, July 11, 2019. www.rollcall.com/2019/07/11/nearly-10-billion-will-be-spent-on-political-ads-in-2020/.
5. Rhonda Ortiz, and Manuel Pastor. "Making Change How Social Movements Work and How to Support Them." University of Southern California, March 2009. https://dornsife.usc.edu/assets/sites/242/docs/making_change_executive_summary.pdf.
6. Latino Decisions. "Latinos Contacted by Campaign or Candidates Nearly Twice as Likely to Vote Early in Election 2018." *Latino Rebels*, October 30, 2018. www.latinorebels.com/2018/10/30/latinoscontacted bycampaign/.
7. Jason Silverstein. "Who Is 'the Squad'? What You Need to Know About Ocasio-Cortez, Omar, Pressley and Tlaib." *CBS News*, July 16, 2019. www.cbsnews.com/news/who-is-the-squad-what-you-need-to-know-about-aoc-ocasio-cortez-omar-tlaib-pressley/.
8. McKay Coppins. "The Billion-Dollar Disinformation Campaign to Reelect the President." *The Atlantic*, February 10, 2020. www.theatlantic.com/magazine/archive/2020/03/the-2020-disinformation-war/605530/.
9. C.N.K. "Digital Disinformation Is Destroying Society but We Can Fight Back." *The Economist*, January 17, 2020. www.economist.com/openfuture/2020/01/17/digital-disinformation-is-destroying-society-but-we-can-fight-back.
10. Donie O'Sullivan. "Zuckerberg Said Facebook Helped Black Lives Matter. Activists Disagree and Are Bracing for 2020." *CNN Business*, October 24, 2019. www.cnn.com/2019/10/24/tech/black-lives-matter-facebook-2020/index.html.
11. Lisa Kaplan, and Ari Shapiro. "How Political Campaigns Can Fight Disinformation." *NPR*, February 10, 2020. www.npr.org/2020/02/10/804616680/how-political-campaigns-can-fight-disinformation.
12. Abby Budiman, Mark Lopez Hugo, and Luis Noe-Bustamante. "Where Latinos Have the Most Eligible Voters in the 2020 Election." *Pew Research Center*, January 31, 2020.
13. Suzanne Gamboa. "Which Democratic Candidate Will Win the Latino Vote? Nevada Is the First Test." *NBC News*, February 17, 2020. www.nbcnews.com/news/latino/which-democratic-candidate-will-win-latino-vote-nevada-first-test-n1137581.
14. Steve Phillips. "12 States Where Democrats Could Flip the Senate." *The Nation*, January 23, 2020. www.thenation.com/article/politics/senate-race-democrats-2020/.
15. "Latino Vote Project." *America's Voice*, April 2019. https://americasvoice.org/wp-content/uploads/2019/04/Latino-Vote-Project-Report.pdf.

7 How We Politicize Our Movements to Build the Country of Our Dreams

Jennifer Epps-Addison

Four years ago, Julius was driving through a North Texas town when the police stopped him, asked him to get out of the car, and told him he was being arrested. When he asked why, the police became violent and accused him of resisting arrest.

That moment stayed with Julius. It inspired him to advocate for transformation of our criminal legal system to end the targeting of and violence against Black people. In 2018, he began to organize with the Texas Organizing Project (TOP) to help to elect local and state officials who would value Black lives through their priorities and policies.

Fourteen years ago, Madai came to the United States in search of freedom and safety. Having a disability and being undocumented makes her an easy target for the Trump administration, but rather than hide in the shadows, she joined CASA in Action to fight for herself and her community. Though she can't vote herself, Madai helped thousands of eligible voters cast their ballots by making phone calls, educating her community, and challenging candidates to adopt plans that protect immigrants like her.

Julius and Madai represent the millions of Black and Latinx people committed to defeating Trump agenda. While their stories are unique to them, their experiences of exclusion, fear, and marginalization are shared by many of us.

Community organizations like TOP and CASA in Action help turn individual experiences into collective power. They are democracy in action—bringing people together across hopes, dreams, struggles and disappointments to demonstrate that our lives are interconnected and that our collective voice in advocating for change is more powerful than acting alone. Together, we can hold politicians and candidates accountable—and elect those committed to justice.

The organization where I am co-executive director, CPD Action, and our sister network, the Center for Popular Democracy, is a network of community organizations. Since we were founded eight years ago, our affiliates have won hundreds of state and local policy victories, impacting tens of millions of people. It has long been our theory that change happens from the ground up by growing and trusting the leadership of those who are most impacted by systems of oppression. The election of Donald Trump has challenged this long-held belief. Under his administration, living in a progressive city is no longer enough to protect our communities. In this moment where our communities are facing relentless attacks, we must politicize our movements and contest for power not just in our local neighborhoods, but as a community of action across the entire nation.

In 2020 our network will join other community organizing networks and movements for justice in the fight for the heart and soul of America by engaging in national and multi-geography political power-building. We have built a federal agenda worthy of our families, and we will bring the power of each of our 53 community-based organizations to the center of politics from our local mayoral elections to the presidential race.[1]

This political moment provides community organizations who have spent more than a decade growing in scale and impact the opportunity to prove ourselves to be electoral powerhouses. In the fall of 2018, Julius worked with TOP to elect a district attorney who ran on ending mass incarceration.[2] Elsewhere in the state, TOP helped to elect 17 Black women as judges in Harris County. Because of their year-round organizing of Black and Latino communities in Texas, TOP turned out 465,000 voters, including 270,000 unlikely midterm voters in 2018.

The years of work from organizations like New Virginia Majority flipped Virginia[3]—Republicans lost six seats in the House and two in the Senate, and Virginians voted in three reform prosecutors. Make the Road Action Nevada grew their canvass program from zero to 30,000 doors in 2018, and their members went on to win housing protections for tenants and worker justice provisions. Detroit Action will build on state victories by knocking on 60,000 doors in must-win Michigan, where Trump won by less than 11,000 votes. In Arizona, Living United for Change in Arizona (LUCHA) knocked on 250,000 doors in 2018—and is prepared to knock on 350,000 in 2020. Through year-round relational organizing, they've led the charge on paid sick day legislation in Arizona and won a ballot initiative to raise the minimum wage.

The year-round effort to knock on doors, register voters, and advocate for public policy that centers our communities is transforming our cities and states. But perhaps more significantly, it is showing Black and Latinx voters that change is possible when we are a part of movements for social change bigger than ourselves.

This hope—this living and breathing example of democracy—is the antidote we need to combat suppression, isolation, and fear. Much has been made about falling Black and Latino voter turnout in 2016, but community organizations have proven time and time again that electoralizing our movements can make history. In making an endorsement,[4] we are showcasing the promise of community organizations for progressive victory up and down the ballot.

A candidate alone cannot build a movement. Speeches can inspire, platforms can spotlight strong policy. Yet campaigns are primarily focused on getting one person voted into power, not on developing the voice of people who have been silenced. Community organizations are the best vehicles for connecting leaders to the people who most need representation and voice.

The candidates that we associate with building movements—Beto O'Rourke in his 2018 Senate bid, Rashida Tlaib and her 2018 House victory—were in deep relationship with community organizations like the Texas Organizing Project and Detroit Action. Though simplified narratives might credit their charisma or strategy for successful campaigns, they did not do it alone.

We know that the stakes are too high in 2020 for Black and Latino voters to be on the sidelines. Our votes are the key to electing a progressive Democrat to the White House. For us to defeat the Trump agenda, we need a movement that represents us and a candidate connected to it.

We're not scared, and we're not turning back. We deserve political candidates worthy of our families. Through our collective action, we can breathe life into our democracy and create an America where we are free to thrive together.

Notes

1. Center for Popular Democracy. "Protecting Our Workers, Sustaining Our Communities: Federal Policy Platform." https://populardemocracy.org/sites/default/files/Protecting%20our%20Workers%2C%20Sustaining%20our%20Communities%20-%20Federal%20Platform%20v3.pdf.
2. Ariel Ramchandani. "A Texas Prosecutor Fights for Reform." *The Atlantic*, October 24, 2019. www.theatlantic.com/politics/archive/2019/10/can-john-creuzot-reform-texas-prosecution/600592/.

3. Tram Nguyen. "Democrats Could Learn a Lot From What Happened in Virginia." *New York Times*, November 6, 2019. https://nyti.ms/2PQ5or6.
4. Daniel Marans. "Influential Progressive Coalition Announces Finalists for Presidential Endorsement." *Huffington Post*, November 11, 2019. www.huffpost.com/entry/center-for-popular-democracy-action-2020-presidential-endorsement-finalists_n_5dca21a9e4b00927b238898a.

8 Rocking the Native Vote

Winona LaDuke

It's 2020, and the stakes are high. In every area of civil society, from the rights of women, the right to clean water, the right to security of home and immigration, to the right to a future, the American election in 2020 will count. Being president of the United States is like being president of the Free World, and, no question, the Trump administration has put the world on edge.

In this upcoming election, every vote matters. (That's even counting that Donald Trump did not win the popular vote in 2016, instead assuming power by winning the Electoral College vote.) Over the past four years, Republican operatives and corporate interests have been pushing to disenfranchise millions of voters, particularly voters of color who would most likely vote progressive. As it turns out, the Native American vote could influence election results in seven major swing states: Arizona, Michigan, Minnesota, Nevada, North Carolina, Wisconsin, and Colorado, according to data from Four Directions, a national Native American research institute.

"We can make a difference," said Renee Lenore Fasthorse Iron Hawk, a member of the Cheyenne River Sioux Tribe in South Dakota. "There are swing states that will make a difference. We can and have mobilized our vote when it matters."[1] 2020 will matter.

The Native American population is 6.8 million, according to the U.S. Census Bureau. While that is relatively small compared with the U.S. population of 330 million, the Native American population has more than doubled its growth rate relative to the general population. From 2000 to 2016, the U.S. population grew 14%, while the American Indian and Alaskan Native population experienced 35% growth. Those Native people are going to vote, and a lot of those people are in rural areas, where Republicans have come to feel comfortable, because Native people have not voted. And a Native candidate, Mark Charles, a citizen of the Navajo Nation, is running for president.

August 2019 saw the first national Native American presidential forum attended by most of the Democratic candidates, except Joe Biden. The Frank LaMere Memorial Presidential Forum was the place to be. It was named in honor of LaMere, who had attended seven consecutive Democratic Conventions until 2012 and was a citizen of the Winnebago Nation. Tribal leaders, journalists, and attorneys put candidates on the spot, asking for some answers and some commitments. Iron Hawk said a new "awakening" of political activism in Native American communities is prompting candidates to respond. Senators Elizabeth Warren, Bernie Sanders, Kamala Harris, and (until he dropped out of the race) former Secretary of Housing and Urban Development Julian Castro all unveiled detailed Native American policy proposals. Senator Amy Klobuchar, despite being from Minnesota, with 11 tribes, did not develop a platform. While most of the attention has been to the lack of funding for basic Native American services, guaranteed under treaty agreements, the reauthorization of the Violence Against Women Act and federal–tribal relations were also key issues. Senators Elizabeth Warren and Bernie Sanders both have come out squarely against the Line 3 and Keystone XL Pipeline projects as a part of both their climate policies, Green New Deal work, and support for Native people. Many candidates supported the reauthorization of the Violence Against Women Act, which allows tribal communities to prosecute nontribal perpetrators—a population responsible for 96% of violent sexual crimes against Native American women.

Native People Are Getting Elected

The historic midterm election of 2018 changed the playing field. That's to say that the election of Representatives Deb Haaland, D-NM, and Sharice Davids, D-KS, brought forward the first Native American women to serve in Congress. In September 2019, Kimberly Teehee became the Cherokee Nation's first delegate to the U.S. House. And in Minnesota, Lieutenant Governor Peggy Flanagan (White Earth Anishinaabe) became the highest elected Native in state office nationally. Elsewhere, Paulette Jordan narrowly lost the gubernatorial election in Idaho, after serving years in the Idaho legislature. Adversity is the norm with Native people, and rocking the vote is one of the antidotes.

Repressing Native Representation

Deprived of the right to vote until 1962 in many states, Native people are just beginning to roll out political power in state and federal elections. "They didn't give us the right to vote until we were 1% of the population," John Trudell, the Santee philosopher and musician, would remind us, noting that if Native people had the right to vote in the 1800s, things might have been different. Native Americans were not citizens of the United States until 1924. When African Americans won citizenship with the 14th Amendment in 1868,[2] the government interpreted the law so it didn't apply to Native people.[3]

"I am not yet prepared to pass a sweeping act of naturalization by which all the Indian savages, wild or tame, belonging to a tribal relation, are to become my fellow-citizens and go to the polls and vote with me," Michigan Senator Jacob Howard told Congress at the time, according to the Native American Voting Rights Coalition.[4]

Native people remain as separate nations but are subjected to state and federal policies that have destroyed sacred sites and people. Native people were only able to win the right to vote by fighting for it state by state. The last state to fully guarantee voting rights for Native people was Utah in 1962.[5] Despite these victories, Native people were still prevented from voting through poll taxes, literacy tests, and intimidation—the same tactics used against black voters. The Voting Rights Act of 1965 helped strengthen the voting rights that Native people had won in every state. However, the act is no longer fully intact. In 2013, the Supreme Court's decision in *Shelby County v. Holder* dismantled one of its key provisions, which required that states with a history of racial bias in voting get permission before passing new voting laws. Just before the 2018 midterm elections, the U.S. Supreme Court ruled in favor of a new voting requirement that may prevent hundreds of Native residents from voting.[6]

Enter North Dakota

During the battle over Standing Rock and the Dakota Access Pipeline, North Dakota state representative Alan Jaeger decided that it was time to deny Native people the right to vote. In this case, the focus was on voters without a street address, that is, those who received their mail at the post office. This is particularly significant in rural counties, where post offices have been closed in budget cuts, but most deeply impacts Native people. Most often tribal housing projects do not have individual postal addresses, but instead most tribal members get their mail at the post office. As the Native American Rights Fund (NARF) explains on its website:

> While North Dakota claims that tribal IDs qualify under its law, most tribal IDs do not have a residential address printed on them. This is due, in part, to the fact that the U.S. Postal Service does not provide residential delivery in these rural Indian communities. Thus, most tribal members use a P.O. Box. If a tribal ID has an address, it is typically the P.O. Box address, which does not satisfy North Dakota's restrictive voter ID law. In both the primary and general election in 2014, many qualified North Dakota tribal electors were disenfranchised because they only had a tribal ID.[7]

NARF originally filed *Brakebill v. Jaeger* in 2016 on behalf of a group of the Turtle Mountain Band of Chippewa tribe, alleging that North Dakota's voter identification law discriminates against Native voters in violation of the Equal Protection Clause and Section 2 of the Voting Rights Act. U.S. District Court Judge Daniel L. Hovland agreed—twice, once in 2016 and again in 2018—and both times issued injunctions blocking portions of the law. In 2018, the Supreme Court ruled against the Native community and for Jaeger, affirming discriminatory voting practices in North Dakota. This ensured, according to court documents, that nearly 2,300 Native Americans were denied voting rights in 2018.

That's when some heroic work began. Native people, infuriated by the continued denial of voting rights, rocked the 2018 election. That's what we saw nationally, with the election of Haaland and Davis, and even more so in North Dakota. Republicans targeted Native voters in North Dakota because the Native vote had been instrumental in electing Heidi Heitkamp as the first woman to represent that state in the U.S. Senate.

North Dakota, after the brutality and militarization of Standing Rock, has well-earned its name as the Mississippi of the North, but the stand-off at Standing Rock seems to have awakened a sleeping giant of Native voters. Native turnout was actually higher than 2012 in several places.[8] The high turnout was not enough to save Heitkamp, as the state's electorate has shifted significantly right of where it was six years ago—but at the state level, angry Native voters flipped at least three red seats blue, including state House Majority Leader Al Carlson.

In the most poetic justice imaginable, Randy Boehning, the four-term state GOP representative who had sponsored the law that disenfranchised Native voters, was unseated by Democrat Ruth Anna Buffalo.

Ruth Anna Buffalo, a Mandan/Hidatsa woman whose lands were drowned by federal policies in the Garrison Diversion Project, became the first Native woman to be elected in the history of North Dakota. That's with the voting rights laws being torn apart. Ruth is in the House. That's why we vote.

Notes

1. Myong, Elizabeth. "Native American Voters Could Help Swing the 2020 Presidential Election." *CNBC*, September 11, 2019. https://www.cnbc.com/2019/09/11/native-american-voters-could-help-swing-the-2020-presidential-election.html.
2. Editors, History com. "14th Amendment." *History*, November 9, 2009. www.history.com/topics/black-history/fourteenth-amendment.
3. Scott Bomboy. "The 14th Amendment's Tortuous Relationship with American Indians." *National Constitution Center—constitutioncenter.org*, March 12, 2014. https://constitutioncenter.org/blog/the-14th-amendments-tortuous-relationship-with-american-indians1.
4. Natalie A. Landreth, Matthew L. Campbell, and Jacqueline De León. "Native American Voting Rights Coalition." *Native American Rights Fund*. Accessed March 29, 2020. www.narf.org/cases/voting-rights/.
5. Library of Congress. "Voting Rights for Native Americans." *Webpage*. Accessed March 29, 2020. www.loc.gov/teachers/classroommaterials/presentationsandactivities/presentations/elections/voting-rights-native-americans.html.
6. Danielle McLean. "New North Dakota Voter ID Restriction Threatens Native Americans' Ability to Vote." *Think Progress*, November 2, 2018. https://thinkprogress.org/exclusive-new-voter-id-restriction-in-north-dakota-threatens-hundreds-of-natives-ability-to-vote-49937a379793/.
7. Matthew L. Campbell, and Jacqueline De León. "Brakebill, et al. v. Jaeger (ND Voter ID Law)." *Native American Rights Fund*. Accessed March 29, 2020. www.narf.org/cases/nd-voter-id/.
8. Stephen Wolf (@PoliticsWolf). "Amazing: Not Only Does It Appear the Backlash to the North Dakota GOP's Discriminatory Voter ID Law Helped Boost Native American Turnout to Historic Highs (Even Higher Than 2008 or 2012 in Some Places!), The Law's Chief Sponsor Lost to a Native American Democrat!" *Twitter*, November 9, 2018. https://twitter.com/politicswolf/status/1060905952583532550.

9 The Resistance Is Fueled by Women

Dana R. Fisher

On the day after the inauguration of Donald Trump in January 2017, the first Women's March took place across the United States and around the world. Although it began as a call to march on Washington, D.C., from a range of individuals on Facebook, the enthusiasm on social media translated into real-world action, and the Women's March mobilized about four million people around the country, becoming the largest protest in U.S. history.[1] The Resistance as a movement really began on that chilly day in January when millions of people—85% of whom were women—joined together to raise their voices to protest the new president and the divisive campaign he ran. Since then, protest events have taken place around the United States, focusing on a variety of issues, including racial justice, climate change, immigration, and the Trump administration's perceived stance on science. In all cases, the participants at these events have been majority woman-identified.

My recently published book, *American Resistance: From the Women's March to the Blue Wave*, presents data collected from thousands of activists who participated in the largest protest events that took place between the inauguration and the midterm elections in 2018.[2] It documents who participated in these events, what motivated them to participate, and what they did after marching in the streets. Combined with interviews with key players who were organizing the Resistance, the book explains how progressive Americans woke up after the 2016 election and what they did afterward. One of the major findings discussed in the book is that the American Resistance is fueled by highly educated, middle-aged White women.[3] This finding is in stark contrast to studies of earlier social movements in the U.S. that found that men are more likely to participate in protest[4] or that there is gender parity in participation.[5]

Resisters did so much more than just march in the streets. Following activists after they participated in these large-scale demonstrations, I document how they went back into their congressional districts and got involved in a whole range of electorally focused activism. Tracing the movement through the 2018 midterm elections, we clearly see how the energy of the activists paid off in a wave of Democratic victories. Resistance groups, many of which were women-led, effectively channeled outrage and enthusiasm in the streets into political action by using "distributed organizing"—a new style of organizing that focuses not on geographic location or pre-existing social ties, but rather on digital connections—to make activism possible by anyone from anywhere, whenever and wherever it is needed most. Thanks to distributed organizing, large-scale protest events have become the start of activism rather than the goal of it. This activism contributed to the Blue Wave that shifted the House of Representatives to Democratic leadership with a group that included more women and people of color than ever before.

In early 2020, there was clear evidence that the Resistance was gearing up to channel the energy and outrage of American progressives into efforts around the 2020 election. However, as federal, state, and local governments respond to the spread of the coronavirus, many questions emerge about how the practice of social distancing will affect activism and efforts to register voters and get them out to participate in the 2020 election. By definition, flattening the curve involves changing the ways that people participate in all sorts of group activities, including campaign events and rallies, voter mobilization and contact, in person activism and protest, as well as in person voting, which frequently involves standing in line. While many states around the United States implemented policies to enable social distancing, I heard from a number of leaders of progressive groups how they are planning to double down on digital tools and distributed organizing techniques to keep their members involved in the election. Numerous groups have released digital toolkits for activists, such as Indivisible, SwingLeft, and many others. Even organizers from the campaign for Elizabeth Warren have made available the tools they used in an open-source format.[6] The question that remains is how effective digital activism that involves no in-person contact will be at sustaining engagement in long-term campaigns, as well as in registering and turning out voters. No question that we will have some of these answers come November 4, 2020.

Notes

1. Erica Chenoweth, and Jeremy Pressman. "This Is What We Learned by Counting the Women's Marches." *Washington Post*, February 17, 2017. www.washingtonpost.com/news/monkey-cage/wp/2017/02/07/this-is-what-we-learned-by-counting-the-womens-marches/.
2. Dana Fisher. *American Resistance: From the Women's March to the Blue Wave*. New York: Columbia University Press, 2019.
3. Putnam, Lara, and Theda Skocpol. "Women Are Rebuilding the Democratic Party from the Ground Up." *The New Republic*, August 21, 2018. https://newrepublic.com/article/150462/women-rebuilding-democratic-party-ground.
4. Doug McAdam. *Political Process and the Development of Black Insurgency, 1930–1970*, 2nd ed. Chicago: University of Chicago Press, 1999; Sidney Verba, Kay Lehman Schlozman, and Henry E. Brady. *Voice and Equality: Civic Voluntarism in American Politics*. Cambridge, MA: Harvard University Press, 1995.
5. A. Schussman, and S. A. Soule. "Process and Protest: Accounting for Individual Protest Participation." *Social Forces* 84, no. 2 (December 1, 2005): 1083–1108. https://doi.org/10.1353/sof.2006.0034.
6. Team Warren. "Open Source Tools From the Warren for President Tech Team." *Medium*, March 27, 2020. https://medium.com/@team-warren/open-source-tools-from-the-warren-for-president-tech-team-f1f27d2c7551.

10 It's About the Next Ten Thousand Years

Bill McKibben

It is a cliché at this point to describe an election as "the most important of our lifetimes." Every election is key—they're how we take stock of where we are as a nation. They're part of a chain stretching into the past and into the future.

But if you wanted to make the argument—and I do—that this year actually is special, the climate crisis might be as good a place as any to start. And that's because it comes with a feature that most political issues don't: a deadline. In October 2018, the world's climate scientists issued a special report, assessing our chances of meeting the targets set at the global climate talks in Paris a few years before. Those targets were modest—they called for attempting to hold the planet's temperature increase to 1.5 degrees Celsius. Since we've already raised the temperature one degree, and that's been enough to melt half the summer sea ice in the Arctic, kill off vast swaths of coral reef, and set big patches of the earth on fire, it's not like the Paris targets are *desirable*. (Desirable was the world many of us were born on to.) They're *crucial*. And if we hope to meet them, the scientists were quite explicit: we have to fundamentally transform our energy systems by 2030. They helpfully defined that fundamental transformation: we need to cut our carbon emissions in half. In ten years.

Anyone who has ever spent time around governments knows that speed is not one of their hallmarks. If we have any hope of meeting that target set for a decade out, we need to be hard at work just about . . . now. If another four years of inaction passes, the chance is over, and with it the planet as we've known it.

The last four years, of course, have been more than a time of annoying stasis—*it's been a period of active regression.* The Trump administration has tried, with a good deal of success, to undercut every environmental law on the books, paying particular attention to climate change. A rogue's gallery of coal lobbyists and oil executives have taken the top jobs in the environmental and energy bureaucracies and used the posts to give their industries free rein across the landscape. Where the Obama administration had scored modest successes—ratcheting up the gas mileage for cars, for instance—they've sprinted in the opposite direction.

Above all, of course, they've removed America from those Paris climate accords, in an act of breathtaking vandalism. It took decades for the international community to reach those agreements, and now the country that has poured the most carbon into the atmosphere is also the only country not engaged in the only global effort to do something about it.

It's not that the Paris accords were so amazing—even the people negotiating them acknowledged at their signing in 2015 that they fell short of the task. Even if all the countries on earth kept their pledges, the mercury would still rise nearly three degrees Celsius. But the calculation was that perhaps once countries began implementing renewable energy on a large scale, they'd find it cheaper and easier than they reckoned, and a virtuous spiral would ensue, allowing much faster progress. At first, it seemed to be working—throughout the last decade the world's engineers kept dropping the price of sun and wind, and the pace of installations started to quicken. But then appeared Trump, who labeled global warming a hoax manufactured by the Chinese and who believed that wind turbines caused cancer. It was as if the road along which we were supposed to be accelerating was suddenly filled with potholes; momentum slowed, not just here but in much of the rest of the world. (The appearance of Trump-like figures in other countries didn't help—Brazil's Bolsonaro, for instance, started opening up the Amazon to intense exploitation, an act as reckless as opening a new fleet of gas-fired power plants.) Having lost three decades to the oil industry's campaign of disinformation, we were now losing time again.

And time, as I have indicated, is the most precious asset here. Most of our problems linger—my entire adult life we've been engaged in the fight to try and provide medical care to Americans. It's infuriating that we haven't done it yet; Trump's efforts to cut back access will, of course, kill many and bankrupt more. But at least they won't make it harder to solve the problem once we finally decide to—the day will come when some president is able to make our country match every other industrialized nation, and the preceding decades will not have made it harder. The climate crisis isn't like that—as a team of scientists reported in November, we're about to cross a whole series of tipping points, ranging from destabilizing Antarctic ice sheets to slowing down vast ocean currents. These are not reversible; no one has a plan for refreezing the poles.

Every election that passes, we lose leverage—this time around our last chance at limiting the temperature rise to anything like 1.5 degrees would slip through our fingers. Which is why we need to register and vote as never before. It's also, of course, why we need to do more than that: many of us are also hard at work this year taking on the big banks that fund the fossil fuel industry, trying to pull the financial lever as well as the political one. And even within the world of politics, we need to do much more than vote: no matter who wins, November 4 and 5 and 6 are as important as November 3; we have to push, and prod, and open up space for the people we work to install in office.

But in the autumn of an even-numbered year, we have a superpower that will wither as soon as election day passes. Our vote is our chance to have a say. In the case of the climate, that is not just about what will happen for the next four years. It's about what will happen for the next ten thousand years.

11 The Coronavirus and Economic Crisis

Motivating Voters
With Public Goods and
Economic Justice

Charles Derber

On January 3, 2020, the White House learned of a new virus that was wreaking havoc in China. Within weeks, the coronavirus had spread to South Korea, Italy, and many other countries, including the United States. It became a household word and set off a public health crisis and economic meltdown, dramatically changing the landscape of the election.

Much remains uncertain about the future of the pandemic and the economy at this writing in April 2020. We don't know how widely the virus will spread, how long it will last, and how many people it will kill. But the state of the nation and the future of the economy will be profoundly affected, with big impacts on the election itself.

Here, we briefly consider the way that opponents of the Trump administration can respond to these crises, beginning with an election campaign focused on delivering public health and economic justice. Democratic Congressional leaders need to show how President Trump failed to respond immediately or adequately to the pandemic and the economic crisis, making them worse. And they must show that an all-out agenda of public goods and economic justice orchestrated by government and curbing corporate greed is at the heart of a new Democratic administration—one that is the best approach to both restoring public health and economic wellbeing, particularly for the working people that Trump abandoned after promising them greatness.

The Coronavirus

Pandemic historians point to the 1918 "Spanish Flu" influenza, a plague that killed 750,000 Americans and more than 50 million people world-wide, as a possible guide to the coronavirus. This massive

The Coronavirus and Economic Crisis 51

public health disaster was heightened by the failure of the United States and other governments to contain it with timely emergency measures.

President Trump is repeating that 1918 failure. In the weeks after he learned of the virus in early January 2020, he tweeted that it was nothing to worry about and would "magically disappear," likely by April.

In its first three years, the Trump administration focused on dismantling Obamacare and defunding the government agencies focused on public health, including the White House office on pandemics, established by Obama. Trump cut the budgets of the Centers for Disease Control and most federal health programs, part of his crusade to shrink all government, turn health matters over to the private sector, and punish the "welfare crowd" sponging off "hard-working American tax-payers."

The conservative philosophy of drowning government in the bathtub carried over directly to Trump's handling of the virus. Conservative leaders have long viewed government intervention for public needs as damaging, especially in health care. Public health is a critical "public good," a concept that the Trump administration and right-wingers have long tried to remove from the public vocabulary, since it suggests a collective need for a common good that cannot be delivered by the market.

The Trump administration's philosophy translated into an immediate denial of the very existence of a public health threat, calling the virus during its early spread "a hoax" engineered by Democrats to bring him down. This reckless rhetoric was accompanied by a failure to coordinate the relevant public health agencies and do the massive early testing essential to mapping and containing the epidemic. President Trump lied about the availability of testing and blinded authorities to the scale of the danger. Pandemic history shows that moving slowly to contain the spread typically undermines future solutions, condemning the society to mass death and to overwhelming public health and economic catastrophes.

The disastrous failure to test early was accompanied by a failure to provide protective masks, sanitizers, ventilators, additional hospital beds and ICUs, and a public information campaign that would alert the public to how to protect themselves and others. In February, health workers, crucial to fighting the pandemic, were sent *without* any protective gear to evaluate patients and then sent home on public transportation and planes, further endangering the public. President Trump said that "the risk was low," repeating the 1918 mantra that this was just another case of the flu. He lied both about the risk of fatality on contact and the degree of spread. Even when he finally acknowledged that the virus was serious, fearful that its economic impact would sabotage his presidency, and even while trying to promote himself as a "war-time president" who would lead Americans to victory, his administration was unwilling and unable, as we show next, to deliver the policies that would solve the crisis.

The Economic Crisis

As the virus quickly spread throughout the world, global and U.S. markets entered a period of volatility that soon evoked predictions of economic catastrophe. Harvard economist and former chair of the Council of Economic Advisors under Obama Jason Furman predicted in March that this would be the greatest U.S. economic crisis since the Great Depression. By mid-March, many economists said a serious national and global recession had already begun and could last months if not years.

The markets and economy had been at risk before the virus emerged. The 10-year market boom beginning in the Obama years had led, in the Trump years, to a speculative bubble in stocks, overvalued at their peak at 150% of their historical relation to corporate earnings. The stock market bubble—fueled partly by corporations using their 2008 bailout money to buy back and inflate their own stock values—was accompanied in the economy by growing, unsustainable levels of debt, both corporate and personal (including massive student debt), a contraction in manufacturing due partly to outsourcing and trade wars, job insecurity, and a level of extreme inequality, parallel to the 1890s Gilded Age, that left millions of working people just $400 away from bankruptcy if they lost a job or had an illness or other family emergency.

These indicators of economic trouble were masked before the virus by top-line official numbers trumpeted by the Trump administration about high stock values and low unemployment levels. But the epidemic revealed and exacerbated the cracks in the neoliberal U.S. system. It highlighted the vulnerability to stock-market and debt bubbles and the suffering of millions of working people living on the edge.

The epidemic triggered a decline in the consumer demand that had fueled the neoliberal economic "boom." As travel by cruise ships and airplanes during the 2020 spring travel season shut down over fear of the virus, creating a huge crisis for the airline and travel industry, the "community spread" of the virus inside the United States forced workers to stay home; canceled business, academic, and other conferences; shut down schools; and ended public gatherings for entertainment and sports events. Essential "containment" measures killed off small businesses, such as restaurants and entertainment businesses, and created crises for low-income workers who were laid off or could not work remotely from home in the way that techies at Google or Facebook could.

Fears about safety prevented millions from purchasing in-person services, intensifying a growing crisis of demand in the huge service sector that traditional monetary or fiscal stimulus policy could not prevent. Millions of workers already on the edge—with millions more now laid off and sinking into poverty—had to stop spending and borrowing, at a scale, if continued, that would destroy the consumer demand that had powered the economy for so long.

President Trump blamed the Federal Reserve as the markets began to tank in February and March 2020. But it was his own policies of massive tax cuts for the biggest corporations and ultra-rich that had set up the potential for the larger crisis among the working classes who had to rein in both borrowing and spending. The Fed responded with emergency cuts, but it had few tools to respond effectively to a massive consumer retrenchment by hard-pressed workers. Interest rates were already extremely low, and even approaching zero would not bring sick workers or indebted small businesses back to life in the new era of the pandemic. Moreover, the Trump administration's trade wars had already disrupted complex, interdependent global supply chains, whether the Chinese-manufactured parts of Apple devices or Ford cars, that threatened by March 2020 to create a supply crisis as well as a demand crisis.

Through both his failure to take the virus seriously, and his oligarchic economic policies for the rich before and during the virus, President Trump helped dig the economic graveyard that might bury his electoral prospects. He sent billions in aid to airlines and other corporations but offered far from adequate help to laid-off workers who desperately needed jobs as well as generous sick leave, unemployment insurance, long-term income support, and more funds for child care, health care, and housing.

But opponents of the Trump administration cannot succeed just by watching Trump fail. They need to offer a clear alternative for saving the country from the pandemic and a new economic approach that can provide all workers employment security and create sustainable and more egalitarian economic growth.

Strategies for Winning the Election and Solving the Public Health and Economic Crises

Opponents to Trumpism can gain the trust of the people only by offering an unprecedented and credible program of funding mass public health and other public goods, as well as a huge array of working-class economic justice policies to end the viral threat and bring the economy back from collapse. At the heart of both sets of policies is a recognition of the vital importance of public goods and government. This will require focus on the needs of working people rather than the corporations who have gotten fat off the bailouts in the 2008 Great Recession and even fatter from President Trump's trillions in corporate welfare and tax cuts.

Democratic Congressional leaders should educate the public about the coronavirus as a lesson in the necessity of public goods and the need for government to protect ordinary people and stop corporate theft of the nation's wealth. They need to attack President Trump on his de-funding of public goods, especially the public health infrastructure, and of government generally, a message which the coronavirus will make seem not Leftist claptrap but common sense.

Health care was already a central issue in the campaign, as the Trump administration has eviscerated the protections of Obamacare. Even before the virus, this led centrist Democrats, including Joe Biden, to advocate not only for restoring Obamacare but adding a "public option," the first step toward a more comprehensive public health system that the virus has made an absolute moral necessity.

Everybody is now dependent on a massive building of a public health structure that can save lives from this and future pandemics. As in the AIDS crisis of the 1980s and 1990s, it will take an all-out movement of the most vulnerable communities and workers to insist on a public health response up to the task, one tied to a huge government investment in the health care sector and affected populations that can prevent another Great Depression and keep millions from dying of the coronavirus.

The virus may, indeed, create the best historical moment for progressives to achieve their agenda by defining themselves as the national voice of public health and public goods, as Trumpists fail to deliver because they seek policies mainly to protect the wealthy. But progressives will fail if they assume that the Trump administration's failures will assure them victory. They have to credibly prove they have a better agenda to halt the virus and preserve public health.

A similar moment is arriving in the economic crisis. The essential role of government becomes most clear during economic crises, with government the most powerful force to protect working people from the perils of an oligarchic economy based on extreme inequality. Trumpism won over industrial voters in swing states like Wisconsin, Pennsylvania, and Michigan who were imperiled by corporate trade agreements, outsourcing, and union-busting. But President Trump made conditions worse for workers by passing massive tax cuts for the wealthy, degrading working conditions by attacking unions, cutting social welfare programs, and deregulating banks and consumer protections.

The economic crisis—perhaps the worst in American history—provides an exceptional opportunity in the 2020 election for Democratic leaders to present a pragmatic but transformational class-based politics, which has become a matter of survival for millions of working people. The new class-based approach must highlight, like Franklin D. Roosevelt's New Deal, the essential role of government in protecting workers and saving the economy, by investing massively in infrastructure, jobs, and long-term support of worker income and benefits. (The Danish government is paying their entire national workforce six months of income support funneled through businesses that keep them employed.) The Democrats must show that the Trump administration has betrayed working people, *and* that they have a real plan to save the working classes.

As Joe Biden likes to say, here's the deal: massive increases in spending on scientific health research and broader public health infrastructure to combat the coronavirus and future viruses; a Green New Deal, guaranteeing training and new green jobs to workers in fossil fuel and all other industries and services, as we transition toward a green infrastructure; and an increase in public goods—including food and housing for low-income workers and the unemployed. This includes major new public investments in social security, health care, and affordable education; reduction or cancellation of student debt; and mandated income support, generous sick leave, housing, child care, and elder care.

By bailing out the banks without bailing out workers, Obama did not advance this opportunity for a Democratic, labor-based strategy to protect workers rather than corporations. Despite his promise, and some plans for a trillion-dollar stimulus, none of Trump's policies are up to the monumental task of saving the economy and helping the most vulnerable workers and victims of the virus. President Trump and conservative Republicans will never invest in the workers, people of color, women, and other vulnerable populations, since they want to use government to enrich themselves and their billionaire donors. They will continue to reject social welfare and massive essential public investment in jobs, as in the Green New Deal.

The Trump administration bailout of Spring 2020 helped the rich as in 2008—saving corporations like Boeing through grants and subsidies and new bailouts, which corporations will once again, overcoming minor legal hurdles, use to buy back stock, raise executive compensation, lay off workers through outsourcing and robotics, and donate to re-electing corporate conservatives. These are the "benefits" of the Fed's unregulated multi-trillion-dollar loans and subsidies to big companies. President Trump's checks to workers will temporarily alleviate the pain of some workers and communities, but they are sugar-highs that will never be remotely enough to protect the population and change the underlying inequality and corporate-friendly tax policy fueling the spread of the virus.

Anti-Trumpists, both progressives and centrists, must seize the moment to call for massive public investment in health, jobs, and green infrastructure. Senators Bernie Sanders and Elizabeth Warren have promoted this new vision in a transformative way, with Warren, after dropping her bid for presidency, showing how anti-Trumpists need to expose the new bailouts in the Trump administration policies as corporate giveaways. She has demanded stipulations that no corporate relief can be used for stock buybacks, executive pay, deregulation, and the like. Sanders and Warren have helped push both progressives and moderates toward more progressive policies. Biden, despite his enormous faults, has moved beyond Obamacare to a public option; he has promised $1.7 trillion dollars to address climate change and create green jobs; and he promises race and gender justice in a multi-generational, multi-racial economic agenda for jobs and working people.

Progressives must help shape an extremely progressive message that is simply pragmatism in the era of the coronavirus.

Why will a Democratic administration, even under a Biden leadership, probably push a progressive agenda to a surprising degree? The new dire circumstances—and the insanity and sociopathy of the Trump Administration years—has made a new class politics for labor unifying and practical. It is the economic side of the public goods agenda necessary to protect the public and promote economic justice in an age of extreme inequality and extreme health and economic peril for workers as well as students and the elderly.

It also happens to be the agenda that has the best chance to turn out massive numbers of women, students, people of color, and white workers. In other words, it is the turnout strategy now essential for anti-Trumpists to beat the Trump agenda. It is also the turnout strategy to create a newly bold government that most Americans will embrace because they need it desperately—literally now a life and death issue—for their health, jobs, and community.

There are no guarantees the Democratic establishment or leadership will itself rise to the task. After the crisis could no longer be denied, President Trump led daily health and economic briefings, political pep rallies in which he made absurd claims about how he was promoting perfect health and economic policies. Early on, leading Democratic officials remained surprisingly quiet, failing to assert the alternative Democratic agenda that would ensure both public and economic health. President Trump's approval numbers actually began to rise by mid-March.

Anti-Trumpists will fail if they assume the huge crisis will bring the Trump administration down; it could raise him up. The only winning approach is to vocally assert an unprecedented public investment in public health, jobs, and the environment, while protecting especially the most vulnerable. That program will have to be far more robust than even FDR's New Deal, because the crisis itself is more serious than the Great Depression.

Take heed! Crisis may reflect opportunity, but only by embracing the courage and vision to act with the never-before-seen boldness and vision to actually solve this terrifying crisis.

12 Get Out the Vote for a World Beyond Fossil Fuels

Annie Leonard

As the 2020 election approaches, we find ourselves in a state of emergency. An emergency for our democracy, for the most vulnerable among us who have suffered the brunt of Trump's attacks, and for our shared climate. This last emergency—the global climate emergency—is a crisis unlike anything we've seen before. Because it's not just a challenge for our country, and, really, it's not even a single challenge. It's a product of rampant capitalism, colonialism, structural inequality, and corporate greed centuries in the making. And we need big, bold, systems-wide solutions to address it.

If our politicians don't get serious about the climate emergency in 2020, we will simply run out of time to protect those who stand to lose the most. For the past several elections, even the politicians who claim to care about our future have done little more than say they believe climate change is real. That talking point doesn't cut it anymore. True climate champions have to take bold, ambitious action. If we are all going to make it out of this crisis, we the people must take back power from the fossil fuel industry and its enabling politicians—2020 is the year our movement must demand a reckoning.

Scientists and activists have been warning us for decades that if we failed to stop burning fossil fuels like oil, gas, and coal, we risked severe and escalating climate impacts. In 2020, that moment arrived. Record-breaking heat waves, wildfires, and superstorms make weekly headlines. Millions of species face extinction. The combined impacts of fossil fuel pollution and climate-fueled disasters disproportionately hit Black, Brown, Indigenous, and working-class communities. Climate-linked extreme weather events have cost the global economy $650 billion over the last three years and are fueling conflict, displacement, and humanitarian crises around the world.

The fossil fuel industry—oil corporations like Shell, Exxon, Chevron, BP, and their friends—have known their business depends on being able to pollute for free for a long time. That's why they've spent billions of dollars on lobbying and misleading PR campaigns to block climate action. Fossil fuel companies want you to believe that they are inevitable. They want to limit our imagination of a cleaner, healthier, more just world. They want us to accept politicians that deny climate change, turn their backs on inequality, and pass laws that give breaks to the wealthy and well-connected while taking away rights from those on the margins.

With the consequences of climate change becoming impossible to ignore, polluting oil companies are desperate for us to believe they are somehow part of the solution. The truth is that they caused this crisis, knew the truth, lied about it, and are continuing to fuel a global emergency while casting themselves as saviors. Having been called out for their outright climate denial, in 2020 they're shifting to a new tactic: delay. They're publicly pushing false solutions to the climate emergency while quietly planning a trillion-dollar expansion to drill and frack us into oblivion. What fossil fuel executives don't want you to know is that they've already discovered five times more oil, gas, and coal reserves than we can afford to burn if we hope to avoid the worst impacts of climate change. Make no mistake, there is no "solution" to the climate emergency that includes continuing to dig up and burn fossil fuels.

Climate denial is not a victimless crime, and this election is our chance to hold the perpetrators accountable. Come November, we can choose a different path forward. But we have to show up at the polls and in the streets, and we have to bring everyone we know who cares about climate justice along with us.

Taking on the climate emergency is a big job, and if we've learned anything in the past four years, it's that the person sitting in the White House matters a lot. We deserve a world beyond fossil fuels: a world in which workers' rights, community health, and our shared climate come before oil company profits. And our next president has a chance to lay the groundwork.

A climate president could stop all new fossil fuel extraction. That should start on day one with an executive order to stop new oil, gas, and coal leasing on our public lands, which already accounts for 24% of U.S. carbon emissions. They can also ban climate-wrecking crude oil from being shipped overseas. And they could restore the 95 (and counting) environmental protections Trump and his cabinet of industry lobbyists have tried to gut—policies like the Endangered Species Act, the Clean Water Act, and the National Environmental Policy Act.

A climate Congress could pass a Green New Deal, transforming the basis of our economy from extraction and exploitation to community-powered, renewable energy. They can prioritize justice and equity for those historically affected by fossil fuel pollution and climate impacts, ensuring the renewable energy revolution leaves no one behind. And they can initiate a just transition for fossil fuel industry workers, one that guarantees comparable wages and job training in new fields that will restore ecosystems rather than destroy them. If we get it right, the transition to a renewable energy economy can not only reduce greenhouse gas emissions by 80%, but also add 550,000 jobs each year while saving the U.S. economy $78 billion through 2050.

Climate governors, state legislators, city councils, and mayors could transform our energy systems to run on renewable electricity, prioritize environmental justice by cleaning up pollution in working-class communities, expand equitable access to public transportation, and revamp building codes to make our homes and workplaces healthier, safer, and more efficient.

This future is within our reach, but corporate greed and cowardly politicians are standing in the way. No matter who the next president is, we know that oil corporations will throw their weight behind blocking climate action, having deceived the public for decades about who they are and what they stand for. They will be ready to tell whoever gets elected in November that the change we want—the one science demands—is too much, too fast, and too risky. They have money, but we have people power on our side. It's up to us to make sure our politicians look those executives directly in the eye and tell them their time is up.

The first step happens at the ballot box when we come together to vote for climate champions.

To help you and your family, friends, and neighbors choose climate champions this year, Greenpeace has ranked every presidential candidate on their climate platforms. We've pored over every plan and every policy the candidates have released on climate to help you decide which one is best positioned to confront the fossil fuel industry and pave the way for a Green New Deal. While everyone has room for growth, it's worth noting that Donald Trump is the only candidate to score zero out of a possible 100 points, an "F." We're also participating in the No Fossil Fuel Money pledge, calling on candidates to refuse all money from fossil fuel PACs, executives, and registered lobbyists. It's time for everyone running for office to recognize that this industry—whose business model is planetary destruction—no longer deserves a voice in our politics.

If you're fired up, you don't have to wait for November to make your voice heard. Start organizing today! You can get involved with the youth-led global climate strike movement; host a Fire Drill Friday rally in your community; help your friends, neighbors, and family make their plans to vote; and volunteer to help others turn out to the polls. Head to greenpeaceusa.org and we'll help you get started.

We're at a turning point. Every one of us must decide if we want to be on the side of climate justice or the side of the fossil fuel companies watching the world burn for their profit. I believe the side of justice will win. We can stop Shell, Exxon, Chevron, and BP from drilling and fracking us into collapse. We can pass a Green New Deal and create a just, equitable future for ourselves and our children. But we can only do it if we all get out and vote in November.

13 Your Vote Can Help Move U.S. Foreign Policy From Militarism to Diplomacy

Medea Benjamin

For young people in this country who have just come of voting age, they have lived their whole lives in a nation at war. Just let that sink in. The 9/11 attacks have been followed by 18 years of war—and counting. The youth of this country have also been robbed of free college education, a decent health care system, and the funds needed for a Green New Deal because over 50% of this nation's discretionary funds are siphoned off to the Pentagon budget. Voting in new leaders is no guarantee that peace will break out or that the military budget will be right sized, but keeping Trump in the White House and a Republican-controlled Senate is a guarantee that the military-industrial complex will remain in the driver's seat, keeping this nation on the warpath. If people come out in record numbers in the next election and vote for a real alternative, we could not only transform our nation internally, but transform the way the United States relates to the rest of the world.

After the 9/11 attacks, the past two decades of war have been, for the most part, bipartisan disasters. George Bush, a Republican president, got us into the quagmire in Afghanistan, but every congressperson except Barbara Lee voted for it. Many lives and $2 trillion later, the Taliban control more territory than they did 18 years ago, and corruption in the U.S.-backed Afghan government is endemic. George W. Bush dragged us into the quagmire in Iraq, which unravelled that nation and led to the rise of ISIS. Forty percent of Democrats in the House and 58% of Democratic Senators voted for this disastrous war.

In the 2008 presidential election, the American public had already turned against the Iraq war, and Barack Obama gained an edge over Hillary Clinton because of his opposition to it. Many voters expected him to be a "peace president," and to his credit, his administration heralded two very important foreign policy breakthroughs: the signing of the Iran nuclear deal and the establishment of diplomatic relations with Cuba. Other than those two achievements, however, Obama continued most of the conflicts that he inherited and started new ones, such as the tragic invasion of Libya.

Donald Trump also ran on a populist anti-war platform, railing against George W. Bush for dragging our nation into the Iraq war, which he has called "the worst single mistake ever made in the history of our country." Even in office, Trump continued to talk about the need for the United States to "get out of these ridiculous, endless wars, many of them tribal, and bring our troops home."[1] He made a short-lived attempt to end the U.S. military presence in Syria, pushed talks with the Taliban in Afghanistan, and began an unsuccessful dialogue with North Korea.

Yet, for most of his time in office, Trump has been a hawk. For all his talk about bringing our troops home, he sent almost 20,000 more to the Middle East and upped the air wars. He brought dangerous warmongers such as John Bolton and Mike Pompeo into top positions in government. After he finally fired Bolton, Trump quipped that if he had listened to Bolton, "We would have been in World War Six by now." We might not be headed to World War Six, but Trump's rash behavior on the world stage could well take us into World War Three.

The Trump administration's worst foreign policy has been its belligerence toward Iran. Whether it wanted to undo Obama's accomplishments or do the bidding of Israel and Saudi Arabia, Trump tore up a nuclear agreement that was working and was supported by the global community. He imposed brutal sanctions on Iran that have decimated its economy and brought hardships to millions of ordinary people. Then, on January 2, 2020, he ordered the assassination of Iran's top commander, General Qassem Soleimani, which brought us to a dangerous precipice that could lead to war at any moment.

This is one of the reasons that the upcoming election is so critical. In the case of Iran, it could literally make the difference between war and peace.

After two decades of constant conflict, the American people are sick and tired of war. A 2019 Pew Research Center poll found that 62% of Americans said the war in Iraq was not worth fighting, and 59% said the same for the Afghan war.[2] There is even less support for a war with Iran. A September 2019 University of Maryland poll showed that a mere one-fifth of Americans said the United States "should be prepared to go to war" to achieve its goals in Iran, while three-quarters said that U.S. goals do not warrant military intervention.[3]

A new presidential agenda could lead to the transformational, progressive foreign policy we so desperately need. So, what are the elements of such a policy?

In broad strokes, it would be a policy that jettisons the imperial framework of "American exceptionalism" and instead respects the sovereignty of other nations. It would be a policy that focuses on international cooperation, conflict prevention, and peacebuilding. It would be a policy based on the same values of human rights and justice that we seek at home, including lifting people out of poverty, empowering workers, and combating the catastrophic effects of climate change.

It would insist on the safe and orderly withdrawal of all U.S. troops from Afghanistan, Iraq, and Syria, and an end to U.S. air wars. Yes, getting out of entrenched U.S. entanglements will be messy, but it can certainly be carried out in a more effective way than the unplanned, uncoordinated, and erratic actions in Syria, which gave a green light for Turkey to slaughter the Kurds. U.S. withdrawals must be coordinated with our allies and be part of diplomatic processes.

A new course of action is particularly urgent in the cases of Iran and North Korea. In the case of Iran, this means rejoining the nuclear deal, lifting the brutal sanctions, and beginning a process to normalize relations. With North Korea, we must replace the current armistice with a real peace treaty that would finally put an end to the 1953 Korean war. We must stop the provocative military exercises with South Korea, lift the economic sanctions, and begin economic cooperation. Only then will the North Korean leadership be willing to dismantle their nuclear weapons.

Revamping our foreign policy also means revamping our overseas alliances, including U.S. support for autocratic regimes. Saudi Arabia, one of the most repressive and dangerous regimes on earth, has shamefully become a key U.S. partner and the number one purchaser of U.S. weapons. The U.S.-backed Saudi-led war against Yemen has led to the world's greatest humanitarian crisis. The United States must stand up to the weapons dealers by demanding an end to all arms sales to the kingdom. It should sanction Saudi leaders involved in the murder of journalist Jamal Khasshoggi, including Crown Prince Mohammad bin Salman. And it should pressure the Saudi regime to release Saudi women activists; respect the rights of free speech and free assembly; stop spreading its intolerant perversion of Islam, Wahhabism, around the world; and most important, end the war in Yemen.

Our unconditional support of Israel also needs to end. The United States provides $3.8 billion of taxpayer money to the Israeli military every year and protects Israel diplomatically in the United Nations so that Israel is never held accountable for its inhumane treatment of Palestinians. While the pro-Israel lobby continues to hold enormous sway in the White House and halls of Congress, public opinion toward Israel is changing dramatically, especially among young people inside and outside the Jewish community. Several Democratic senators, including Bernie Sanders and Elizabeth Warren, have called for conditioning U.S. aid to Israel on respect for human rights and adherence to international law. We must stop giving Israel a blank check to commit war crimes, but we must also get real about solutions. Instead of mouthing platitudes about a "two-state solution" that has become impossible due to Israel's ever-expanding settlements or giving credence to Trump's ridiculous Peace Plan that has absolutely no Palestinian support, we need to focus on a policy based on rights and equality for all.

Our efforts to wind down U.S. intervention in the Middle East should not be used as a pretext for ramping up conflicts elsewhere, particularly with Russia and China. The anti-Russia sentiment that has emerged with the allegations of Russian interference in U.S. elections, the increased sanctions on Russia, and the U.S. withdrawal from the INF nuclear treaty have led to a dangerous Cold War-like atmosphere.

The same is true with China, where U.S. officials portray China as an economic adversary, a potential military threat, and a threat to U.S. economic interests with its increasing influence in Africa and Latin America. But viewing Russia and China as threats only justifies more military buildup. We need to stop making new enemies and instead join forces with major powers like Russia and China to help uplift other parts of the world, particularly in the Global South.

That would require the United States to treat countries in the Global South as partners, not countries we bully, threaten, occupy, and exploit. This is true for Africa, where the United States has been expanding its military presence, but particularly true in Latin America, where the United States has a history of domination and the Trump administration has openly resuscitated the imperial Monroe Doctrine.

A progressive foreign policy would not support governments—anywhere in the world—that come to power through coups, such as the case of Honduras in 2009 or more recently Bolivia. It would re-establish full diplomatic relations with Cuba and would lift economic sanctions on Venezuela, Nicaragua, and Cuba. It would support grassroots, community-based organizations that are empowering the poor and most marginalized sectors of society, and cooperate with governments and nongovernmental groups to address the climate crisis.

It would also be generous with humanitarian aid and more supportive of refugees, especially people who are fleeing violence that our government had a role in creating. It would lift the Muslim ban and end the inhuman treatment of migrants at the U.S.–Mexico border.

Revamping our foreign policy would also require a re-examination of the need for U.S. military bases overseas. The United States is the only country in the world with hundreds of foreign bases (over 800!), spread across more than 90 countries. Many bases are relics of the Cold War and have no strategic value today. In some countries, local opposition has generated anti-American sentiment that jeopardizes our security. Some bases, like the ones surrounding Iran, are sitting targets should there be an outbreak of hostilities. A progressive foreign policy would close most of our military bases abroad and take responsibility for cleaning up the contamination caused by the military's reckless use of hazardous materials.

Another area that desperately needs radical change is our nuclear weapons program. The United States has over 7,000 nuclear warheads, more than any other nation on earth, and has refused to implement existing disarmament commitments in the 1970 Nuclear Non-Proliferation Treaty (NPT), which requires all nuclear weapons states to move toward "full and complete nuclear disarmament." A great boon to global nuclear disarmament would be for the United States to join the new UN Weapons Ban Treaty and to scrap the Obama-era commitment for a massive upgrade to the U.S. nuclear arsenal—a commitment that fuels the arms race and will cost the U.S. taxpayer over a trillion dollars.

Along these lines of saving billions while actually making the world safer, a progressive foreign policy would require massive cuts in the Pentagon budget. From the White House, Trump boasts that he alone has restored the U.S. military to greatness after it was supposedly decimated by Barack Obama (even though Obama continued the bloated Pentagon spending). Trump's 2020 budget of $740 billion is the largest since World War II, which means that it is more than the amount spent on the military during the Korean War, the Vietnam War, or the height of the Reagan buildup. He brags that this buildup will create tens of thousands of jobs, but studies show that the Pentagon is actually a poor job creator. Money put into public education would create twice as many jobs, and shifting $125 billion a year from the Pentagon to green manufacturing would result in a net increase of 250,000 jobs.

From Militarism to Diplomacy 67

As an alternative to the present budget, the Poor People's Campaign came out with a detailed report, "Poor People's Moral Budget: Everybody Has the Right to Live,"[4] showing how we can extract ourselves from harmful systems and invest in rebuilding our failing infrastructure, create jobs, provide health care and housing, and alleviate poverty. It calls for a cut of $350 billion in annual military spending to fund these needs, which would still leave us with a military larger than China, Iran, and Russia—combined.

With the upcoming elections, the American people have a chance to move toward a moral budget and a moral international stance.

In Congress, we are already seeing some significant policy shifts that could become law if the Democrats were in control of the White House and Congress. Since the 9/11 attacks, Congress has unfortunately been only too happy to leave war-making to the president, abrogating its constitutional role as the only power authorized to declare war. Thanks to public pressure, starting in 2019 there has been a remarkable shift. Both houses of Congress voted to end U.S. support for the Saudi-led war in Yemen and to prohibit an unauthorized war on Iran. Although Trump vetoed the bills, they offer proof that public pressure can move Congress, including a Republican-dominated Senate, to reclaim its constitutional powers over war and peace from the executive branch. If we remove the obstacle in the White House, these bills would become the law of the land.

Another bright light in Congress is the pioneering work of first-term Congresswoman Ilhan Omar, who recently laid out a series of seven bills called Pathway to PEACE. While her bills will be hard to get passed in Congress, the package lays out a marker for where we should be headed. It also shows how voting to put a committed, energetic Muslim woman in Congress can shake up the status quo.

The presidential election offers our best opportunity to transform our desire for peace into reality. The peace movement has influenced most candidates to say that the United States should rejoin the Iran nuclear deal and most have promised to bring U.S. troops home from the greater Middle East. Most have criticized the bloated Pentagon budget (despite the fact that some regularly vote for it), and some have put forth specific ideas. Elizabeth Warren, for example, has called for the elimination of the Pentagon's slush fund for war spending, the Overseas Contingency Operations, which would save $798 billion over 10 years.

The most effective and committed anti-war champion in the 2020 race was Senator Bernie Sanders. The popularity of his call for getting the U.S. out of its imperial interventions and his votes against 84% of military spending bills since 2013 were reflected in the way other candidates are rushing to take similar positions.

A transformational president in the White House would understand that America should not be fighting fruitless wars that only further destroy the planet, but fighting to save the planet. As Senator Bernie Sanders has often noted, "Maybe—just maybe—instead of spending $1.8 trillion a year on military budgets and weapons of destruction designed to kill each other, we can pool our resources as a planet to fight our common enemy: climate change."

That vision, alone, should be a great incentive to get out and vote for candidates who respond to articulate it.

Notes

1. Balluck, Kyle. "Trump Knocks 'ridiculous Endless Wars' amid US Troop Pullout from Syria." *Text*. TheHill, October 7, 2019. https://thehill.com/homenews/administration/464612-trump-knocks-ridiculous-endless-wars-amid-us-troop-pullout-from-syria.
2. Igielnik, Ruth, and Kim Parker. "Majorities of U.S. Veterans, Public Say the Wars in Iraq and Afghanistan Were Not Worth Fighting." *Pew Research Center (blog)*. Accessed May 29, 2020. https://www.pewresearch.org/fact-tank/2019/07/10/majorities-of-u-s-veterans-public-say-the-wars-in-iraq-and-afghanistan-were-not-worth-fighting/.
3. Telhami, Shibley, and Stella Rouse. "Study of American Attitudes toward Iran, Syria, and Afghanistan." *Critical Issues Poll*. University of Maryland, September 2019. https://criticalissues.umd.edu/sites/criticalissues.umd.edu/files/UMCIP%20Suvey%20Study%20Fall%202019.pdf.
4. Poor People's Campaign. "Poor People's Moral Budget," October 3, 2019. https://www.poorpeoplescampaign.org/resource/poor-peoples-moral-budget/.

14 Rebuilding After COVID-19

Equality, Equity, and a Strong Social Safety Net

Wilnelia Rivera and Katherine Adam

The United States is entrenched in a "war" with COVID-19. Though our enemy is invisible to the naked eye, the virus appears in the public conversation through metaphors around victory and battle, comparisons of ventilators to missile production, and Donald Trump taking the mantle of a "war-time president."

War framing may be apt for the earliest phases of this crisis; we are after all possibly turning to policy measures such as the Defense Production Act to mobilize resources in response to a surprise invasion. But if we care about true relief and recovery for the long term, it is not enough. As we emerge from our immediate public health crisis into a difficult period of economic and cultural recovery of unknown length, what will become our country's longer-term response? Will we put in place long-needed safeguards that create a more equitable, just, and healthy society, or will we further exacerbate inequalities?

Those who in this moment best succeed in communicating and organizing a transformative vision of America will win the 2020 election and set a path for the decades ahead. For progressives, this should mean developing a narrative around COVID-19 that speaks to a potential new coalition that shares a set of fundamental values, paired with a historic turnout effort that aims to expand the electorate in November.

If we can empathize with everyone's historic and emerging epidemic-related hardships—while unifying in our steadfast opposition to rising individualism, authoritarianism, and xenophobia—the dynamics are ripe to create a potentially historic electoral realignment.

Electoral realignments occur when voters organize and/or reorganize into another political party. Such moments in national elections are exceedingly rare. One example was the 1932 election, which ushered in the New Deal. While the election of Barack Obama in 2008 could have been another example, it failed to coalesce and sustain a new electoral coalition and by 2016 over 1,000 Democratic seats were lost across the country and Republicans dominated.

However, since the election of President Trump in 2016—well before this present crisis—movement professionals, activists, candidates, researchers, and pollsters began documenting significant changes to the American electorate. These changes signal the emergence of a new potential political force: Republican-leaning, college-educated suburban women realigning with the Democrats, combined with historically lower-voting Black women, Latinx people, other women of color, and millennials turning out in massive numbers. Galvanizing this coalition will be critical to moving forward a post-COVID-19 vision that supports all people.

Hints of this coalition emerged in the "Blue Wave" of 2018, when Democrats flipped the House by a much larger margin of seats than projected and exceeded the historic turnout levels of the Obama coalition. Experts overlooked the rising disaffection against the Trump administration from college educated, suburban Republican women, and they missed the deep motivation of Black women, Latinx people, other women of color, and millennials to vote as an act of defiance. As a result, Democrats resoundingly took back control of the House of Representatives. This included the upset victories of Congresswoman Ayanna Pressley (MA-07)—who defeated a long-time Democratic incumbent in Greater Boston, Massachusetts—and Congresswoman Lauren Underwood (IL-14), who as a first time candidate prevailed in a contested primary before defeating the Republican incumbent in Naperville, Illinois. Both relied on changing parts of the electorate and driving up turnout of historically low-propensity voters to win.

Many view the pre-COVID-19 2020 Democratic presidential primaries as a setback in this strategy because older and suburban moderate voters were more motivated than the low-propensity, but more progressive, voters we need to turn out in the general election to make a coalition work. These older and moderate voters were not willing to take the perceived risks associated with an Elizabeth Warren or Bernie Sanders nomination. However, the collateral impact of the COVID-19 public health and economic crisis creates a reset button—not around a new candidate, but a new agenda and movement.

The key will be developing a narrative that speaks to the values of the nascent coalition we want to turn out to take a bold vote that is worth the "risk." For decades these electoral groups—though not yet voting in coalition—have been consistent in their support for policies that promote equality, equity, and a strong social safety net. COVID-19 is fundamentally a crisis of these very issues. It has made evident that your ability to combat this pandemic or build a new normal is largely dependent on your zip code, income, and education.

Uneven health care access discouraged many Americans from seeking testing or treatment in the early days of the virus. With 24% of Americans lacking any paid leave,[1] unknown numbers of people went to work sick. This has only been made worse by insufficient medical supplies, a shortage of hospitals beds, and health care labor shortages.

A compelling narrative for the future will bring people together by focusing on the values of community, interconnectedness, and care for everyone. It will also affirm the fact that these values can be embodied in policies and investments that create a stronger country: economic safety nets, deep equitable access to good health care, and safe, just communities for all.

Communicating these values will become difficult as unemployment rises and budgets are cut. Proposed investments in the safety net—particularly the scale of types needed for Medicare for All or universal paid leave—will be painted as roadblocks to economic recovery. It will become harder to ensure equity in the face of conservative efforts to craft policy that provides support only to some, with exclusions of others based on race, gender, immigration status, criminal record, or work requirements.

We need both a movement that believes in "deep democracy" and a political operation that fundamentally understands the extraordinary nature of our times. We must recognize and build off the human, community, and local assets who have been on the front lines of this work. For example, these include the reproductive justice activists and organizations in the South and Midwest battling conservative state legislatures and governors who are using this crisis to continue their assault on safe and legal abortion access, harming low-income people, women of color, and millennials, as well as transgender and gender nonconforming people.

President Trump has his base and conservative movement squarely behind him. All Democratic candidates must be bold in unleashing a movement and political operation that builds and turns out the new coalitions of voters ready for progressive change and to rebuild the United States.

We must also remain even more vigilant in preventing foreign and domestic voter suppression efforts and electoral interference, and it is imperative that we move forward efforts to institute a national mail-in ballot system this November. Our government must balance the safety of all Americans and recognize that our current election system in this context is not equipped to administer a clear, nor safe, election.

The United States is approaching a defining moment. As we look upon this historic crossroads, let us choose the path that brings us together to harness the power of all those who have been denied it. To quote Congresswoman Ayanna Pressley, "Those closest to the pain, should be closest to the power."[2]

Notes

1. Drew DeSilver. "As Coronavirus Spreads, Which U.S. Workers Have Paid Sick Leave—and Which Don't?" *Pew Research Center*, March 12, 2020. www.pewresearch.org/fact-tank/2020/03/12/as-coronavirus-spreads-which-u-s-workers-have-paid-sick-leave-and-which-dont/.
2. Representative Ayanna Pressley. "Rep. Pressley Hosts CBC Delegation for Historic Visit to Greater Boston." *Press Release*, January 15, 2020. https://pressley.house.gov/media/press-releases/rep-pressley-hosts-cbc-delegation-historic-visit-greater-boston.

15 Excite the Vote
It Takes a Community *and* a United Front

Charles Derber

Voting has never been the national past-time in America. While proclaimed as a critical civic duty, voting doesn't excite or turn out the population as much as Friday-night high-school baseball or a Sunday football game. Consider the dismal numbers: only about 54% of eligible U.S. voters historically turn out to vote for president, and about 40% for senators or House representatives in non-presidential election years. This translates into 50 million to 100 milllion nonvoters in the United States, a terrible commentary on American democracy. In contrast, many European societies have 70% or higher turnout rates.

This U.S. low-vote exceptionalism reflects government policy and corporate power, and a long history of elite suppression of the vote, but it also highlights shortcomings in U.S. social movements. Many social movement activists and organizations, seeing the corporate domination of both the Democratic and Republican Parties, have viewed electoral politics as a low priority, a diversion from vital organizing on their own core programs. Moreover, many progressives tend to feel that corporate parties, including the Democratic Party, cannot make the policy change they want.

The consequence is that the United States tends to lack the "united fronts" that, in many European and other Western democracies, bring together progressive activists with labor, social democratic, or green parties to turn out the vote. In the United States, the Democratic Party tries to marginalize anti-corporate and other social justice movements, while the movements frequently write off political parties.

Social movements must recognize that an "united front" strategy can serve their core organizing mission of visionary change, despite dangers of electoral co-optation. The rise of Congresswoman Alexandria Ocasio-Cortez (AOC) and other influential movement-activist-legislators show it is possible to get into electoral politics by participating in and growing "the movements."

Presidents tend to define the center of political gravity and shape what is seen as "respectable" or reasonable. The president's ideological position pulls public debate either rightward or leftward. A moderately liberal president makes progressive or Leftist policies easier to introduce in mainstream politics, as happened with Presidents John F. Kennedy and Lyndon B. Johnson.

This is one of the reasons that a united front politics is possible and can increase the membership and electoral possibilities of a mainstream party, whether led by a progressive or a moderate. It pushes the party toward progressive positions because it is a way of exciting the base and giving them a reason to vote.

European movements have long practiced united front politics. Social democratic parties in Europe work with unions and community organizers to turn out voters for their party. European social movements are more able to gain influence in labor or social democratic parties, and thus advance big structural change through legislative changes, such as passing "codetermination" laws that allow workers to vote for 50% of corporate board members.

A united front approach by Democrats can help them win in 2020. Of course, other parties could also adopt this approach. The polls consistently show that the general population is far more progressive than commonly thought, with large majorities hostile to big corporations and the corruption of money in politics, while also strongly supporting unions, more economic equality, government job and welfare programs, and other progressive aims.

The coronavirus made the need for government obvious, but fear, stoked by big Democratic donors, led primary voters to pick a "stabilizing" or unifying candidate. But even the choice of a centrist candidate can advance a united front approach. Moderates will have to offer people and ideas that can build the beginnings of a united front between the movements, the progressive base, and the moderates, such as suburban women, who will coalesce against Trumpism and advance a long-term progressive agenda.

In Spring 2020, when it became almost certain that Joe Biden would be the Democratic choice, he was forced to move in a notably more progressive direction—supporting Bernie Sanders's free college for students in public universities, promoting Elizabeth Warren's progressive bankruptcy bill protecting consumers and students, promoting a public option for heath care and a major green stimulus plan influenced by Representative Ocasio-Cortez—to mobilize the Democratic base. Moreover, Biden, while still a moderate who will fail to advance many vital progressive ideas, may stop the Republican

Excite the Vote 75

packing of the federal judiciary that is propagating more racist and anti-immigrant judicial decisions. A choice of a woman as his running mate may result in a far more progressive agenda. Turning out Black and White women—both working class and professional—is key to the united front Biden or any moderate needs to beat Trump "like a drum." Corresponding steps could be taken by the presumptive Republican candidate to neutralize any perceived Democratic advantage. In fact, through the stimulus and other plans in response to the crises, the Republican Party and its candidates may also advance their equivalents of a united front approach.

Many activists will be very unhappy with a Biden presidency, but an emergency election is no time for romantic sentimentality or fantasy. In a second term, the likely agenda of a re-elected President Trump will not build the movements but simply crush the Left, increasing far-right and even neo-fascist prospects. While progressives may have to hold their nose to vote for Biden, and should often work against his policies, a strategic united front is survival for progressives in 2020.

The united front approach aligns with a crucial reality about voting. People vote with both their head and hearts, but they don't vote alone. Like all social behavior, they vote as part of a conversation with neighbors, work colleagues, family members, fellow parishioners, and other members of their community. Voting is fundamentally a social act, shaped by others who help make your lives meaningful.

Personal behavior—like voting—is shaped to a very large degree by the extent to which the individual's community is mobilized by the shared excitement and imagination of a better life when the community turns out together.

This translates into the nuts and bolts of getting out the vote. It's all about connection and shared excitement. People vote when they talk to each other or when they go to in-person or digital town halls and come out "turned on" by a candidate and a party vision and their enthused neighbors. In a coronavirus era, these community-building election initiatives will go more online but will remain vitally important in getting people excited to vote.

The failure to vote by millions of Americans is shaped by elite-driven government voting restrictions but also by the failure of progressive movements and the Democratic Party to recognize mass isolation and despair. Low voting reflects the spectator culture of a managed population. People take part by picking up snippets of news on their phones or watching a bit of cable television, a kind of enforced political passivity or "spectatorship" that sustains elite rule.

United fronts serve to wipe out political spectatorship. Democrats would blow out Republicans if their base were part of stronger in-person and online communities and movements coalescing on election day to vote. High nonvoting is a failure of community and of the united front that unites community-based social movements and political parties to seize political power.

It turns out that turnout work is a huge component of the core work of social movements and social justice. Turning out millions of new voters and "turning on" millions of reluctant voters is integral to the progressive agenda of creating strong communities excited by the possibility of major changes in their own lives for peace, economic justice, and social well-being. For millions of people in America, voting is the first step in movement engagement and in creating a massive united front, moving from spectator to creating a more democratic, activist society.

Part III
How We Win

16 Vote Is a Verb
Applying Lessons From Social Science to GOTV

Anat Shenker-Osorio

Voting is a thing we're trying to get people to do—as opposed to an idea or belief we want them to hold. And while voting, mercifully, doesn't require a shift of daily routine, it's an action that has less immediate or tangible ties to the life changes most people seek when they take the trouble to do something different. Nevertheless, once we think of voting as a new behavior we want to instill, we can take a more insightful look at our default assumptions around mobilization and deliver what's proven to work.

In the world I inhabit, examining and attempting to shape political perception and motivation, it's hard to think of any element more intensely studied than voting itself. Where our understanding of people's preferences on issues or candidates rely, almost always, on their self-reporting, studies of what's moved people to cast their vote can be based on checking the actual voter file. This means researchers can see what respondents did—not base conclusions on what they said they'd consider doing.

The following is a summary of core lessons gleaned of a robust body of studies where researchers exposed potential voters to some piece of content (often a direct mail flyer) and examined its impact on getting these viewers to the polls:

1. Talk about voting itself. Even where a target audience and an issue line up perfectly—imagine, for illustration, a message about improving water quality sent to Flint residents—messages that center on the importance of voting have still proven to net greater uptick in participation than those purely about issues. The same goes for candidate-centered Get Out the Vote (GOTV) pitches; getting people to vote is best accomplished by talking about voting.

2. Apply social pressure. Social pressure has a merited bad rap because old school approaches to it included invasive missives like "your neighbors can know whether or not you voted." But subtler forms of this approach work while remaining in alignment with progressive values. Indeed, just activating social norms—"everyone is voting, you should too"—has measurable impact, as does cluing people into the fact that whether they've voted is a matter of public record with a simple "thank you for voting last year" for those to whom this applies.

   Most people conform to the social cues of the group with which they identify. If someone hears that my kin group engages in this kind of behavior, they're much more likely to join in the act. This should give us pause about the common tendency to recite statistics about abysmal voting rates. Well-meaning attempts to induce interest by declaring that some particular group has low turnout or frequently fails to show up likely dampen people's desire to vote. It tells people in that category that voting is not what their kind of people do. These previous findings suggest we ought to question the very label "nonvoter." Calling people this risks undesirable self-fulfilling prophecy. No one who is eligible is a *nonvoter*; they're all voters we haven't yet mobilized!
3. Activate identity to compel action. Asking people to *be a voter* and, better yet, getting them to claim this identity out loud themselves, has proven turnout effects. If you've said you'll go vote, but when the day comes your childcare falls through, you feel unwell, or your boss dumps more on your plate, you may not find a way to do it. If, in contrast, you've claimed the identity *voter*, you're more likely to take the action that allows you to credibly merit that label.
4. Get people to make a plan, and provide details on how to do it. Letting people know the nuts and bolts of where, when, and how they can *be a voter* has proven pivotal to compelling this action. Indeed, getting people to talk through their plan—what time of day they'll go to the polls, how they'll get there, who will be with them, and so on—ups your chances they'll make it all happen.

These findings offer a critical catalog of best practices that call into question many of our default approaches to GOTV. And they have been proven to apply across demographic groups and geographies. But they still leave open some questions we're working out. Most critically, what ought to be the role of positive emotions, like hope and pride, versus negative emotions, like fear, disgust, or anger, in our attempts to get people to be voters?

At this moment in particular, reminding people of the literal life-and-death consequences or showing just how nefarious our opponents are might seem like the obvious answer to get them to vote. This can take the form of "this is our last chance," "the stakes have never been higher for our communities," or "vote before it's too late."

But, recalling that being a voter is most aptly understood as a behavior, not a belief, we may wish to reconsider what we're bringing to the fore for our audiences. Most of us have heard the refrain that fear triggers a "fight or flight" response. But, when it comes to political cues, we're starting to see that leading with fear triggers *fight or freeze*.

Fear-based messaging definitely makes some in our audiences want to lace up their gloves and get in the ring. But those are likely the people already won over—people who have gone beyond voting (for those who are eligible) to additional forms of activism and engagement. This risks leaving the rest of our audiences—especially never-before voters—immobilized. The fear that we've brought to the fore has them wanting to hunker down, not try out a new behavior.

Worse yet, we may have activated their understandable suspicion of civic engagement by offering more proof of just how awful elected leaders can be. So, why bother getting up off the couch, let alone—for many in our base—surmounting the deliberately set hurdles to register and cast a vote? Or we've made our opening line about yet another problem when they have more than enough of their own. Not exactly an inspiring way to induce them to add to their to-do list.

In 2018, MomsRising put forth an unprecedented effort—across channels and tactics, with over 38,000 volunteers—to engage moms in North Carolina and Florida, specifically Black, Latina, Asian American, and Pacific Islander moms—that intuitively brought these questions to the fore.

Using mail, text, phone, digital ads, radio, and events, MomsRising spread the word about being a voter to these moms under a future-inflected, positive refrain. The core messaging we developed—*Be a Voter, Raise a Voter* and *Can'tWait2Vote*—made voting itself the centerpiece, and activated identity to inspire action, applying the aforementioned best practices and attempting to add even more potency to them.

Summary results suggest that these targeted voters turned out at higher rates than people of the same demographics who didn't receive the messaging. In the counties where MomsRising engaged, an additional 2% to 8% of people, over and above the uptick in voting witnessed across the country, turned out. To be sure, a true randomized controlled trial would be required to say more definitively that it was this particular intervention that yielded this result.

Voting behavior is highly correlated to parental voting behavior. In other words, kids whose parents vote are more likely to grow up to be voters. By not just targeting moms but having fellow moms as messengers, with messaging tapping into maternal identity, we took what we know works and turned it up a level.

MomsRising wove the dual identities of *mom* and *voter* into more than their messaging. They made voting more feasible and fun by sending out coloring sheets loaded with localized polling place information and placing treasure boxes full of kid-approved distractions in select spots to make waiting in line with little ones easier. While they couldn't eliminate the barrier of lack of affordable childcare for the moms they were targeting, they could make it less prohibitive by turning voting into a family affair.

Where *Be a Voter, Raise a Voter* formed the core of messaging by mail, *Can'tWait2Vote* featured in social media and a digital ad that beat industry standards for completion rates and positive engagement. This ad featured women of all types repeating the refrain "I can't wait to vote" and other colloquial echoes of it, like "I'm gonna vote so hard!" The dominant emotional note in this ad, made by Art Not War, was positive excitement laced with a hint of anger. If you're going to have a negative emotion mixed into your messaging, the better form is catalytic anger, not fear or frustration.

Across the deep dives I've conducted into persuasion and motivation on various issues and in many contexts, we find over and over again that our chief impediment is not the opposition. Our problem isn't that people do not believe that our ideas are right; it's that they do not believe our ideas are possible. Thus, our task is not so much to persuade toward our solutions and policy preferences but rather to overcome the understandable reluctance to bother taking action when it seems things just keep getting harder and worse.

We have seen, for example, in message testing that the seemingly simple reminder of times we've joined together in cross-racial solidarity and achieved (albeit never complete or even sufficient) progress like civil rights legislation, Social Security, and Medicare helps respondents believe it's worth putting forth the effort to engage today.

Abating this cynicism means we must present examples of real achievements that came of the actions we're now asking our audiences to take. And, even more vitally, it requires that we pay close attention to how much we belabor present day problems. In short, we must ensure that our mobilization efforts give our audiences something desirable to vote *for*, not merely something deplorable to send packing.

17 Latino Voter Outreach That Energizes White Voters, Too[1]

Ian Haney López

My granddaughter is part of a new generation that will swell the number of Latino voters to 32 million this year.[2] Somewhere in the United States, a young Latino turns 18 every 40 seconds, and the Pew Research Center projects that in 2020 Latinos will become the largest non-white segment of the electorate, surpassing African Americans.[3]

Almost two-thirds of Latino voters align with the Democratic Party (62% Democrat compared with 34% Republican), so it seems evident this wave is a boon for Democrats. But there's potential danger as well. Recent research shows that Democratic efforts to woo Hispanics—or, more precisely, certain forms of outreach—can cause liberal white voters to shift their allegiance from Democrats to Republicans.

My own research on racial dynamics in voting confirms this insight. But I've also found that there's a way to galvanize Latino voters that, far from alienating whites, energizes them as well. In a close election, 2020 could well turn on whether—and how—Democrats reach out to Latino voters.

One way to connect to Hispanic voters is to run ads in Spanish. This appeals to voters proficient in Spanish. And even for those who are English-dominant (as are 90% of Latinos born in the United States),[4] campaign ads in Spanish can communicate respect and welcome. But to a disturbing number of white Democrats, Spanish seems to communicate something else entirely.

The research of the political scientist Mara Cecilia Ostfeld highlights the potential risk.[5] Ostfeld conducted a 2012 experiment with almost 600 white adults using a 30-second ad taken from the Obama campaign. Half the group watched the original in English. The other half watched a version in which the audio content was presented in Spanish, supplemented by English subtitles.

Whites who identified as Republicans largely rated Obama poorly. Whether they watched the English or Spanish version mattered little to them.

But among whites who identified as Democrats, the Spanish ad had a significant negative impact. "Levels of favorability toward Obama were about 11 percentage points lower among White Democrats after viewing the ad with Spanish-language content—despite the fact that there were English subtitles and the content was, therefore, fully accessible—relative to when viewing the same ad entirely in English," Ostfeld reported.

Ostfeld found similar negative effects when Democratic candidates were described as "courting" Hispanic voters. In 2016, she showed white adults two versions of an online news headline. One said "Hillary Clinton Courts Undecided Voters." The other declared "Hillary Clinton Courts Latino Voters." When shown the Latino outreach version, white Democrats were about 9% less likely to say they would vote for Clinton, and 11% more likely to vote for Donald Trump. The difference in reaction among white Democrats—currently 59% of all Democratic voters, according to Pew—could swing the 2020 election if this effect were to manifest in the voting booth.[6]

This potential dynamic echoes what I've found with race in electoral campaigns. Many whites have long filtered Democratic efforts to woo African Americans through a zero-sum frame in which they worry that gains for blacks come at the expense of whites.

But a large research project I co-directed along with Anat Shenker-Osorio and Heather McGhee found that there are ways to address race that generate enthusiasm for progressive positions among people of color while increasing, rather than diminishing, support from whites as well.[7]

To study how to talk about race in political campaigns, in 2018 we polled a nationally representative sample of 2,000 people. Among other things, we asked respondents which came closer to their views: a pro-business message or a progressive economic message. The pro-business message said: "To make life better for working people we need to cut taxes, reduce regulations, and get government out of the way."

For the progressive message, we offered respondents two versions. One included the italicized text and the other did not: "To make life better for working people we need to invest in education, create better paying jobs, and make health care more affordable for *white, Black, and brown* people struggling to make ends meet."

The race-silent version of the progressive message beat the pro-business message by a margin of 32 points. This result suggests that voters generally prefer progressive over pro-business economic policies.

But when the progressive policy message included the phrase "white, Black, and brown," the winning margin over the pro-business message increased to 41 points.

Importantly, this included a big jump in favorable response from whites. Hearing that progressive policies would help "white, Black, and brown people" increased white support for investing in education, creating better-paying jobs, and making health care more affordable by 12 percentage points. The inclusion of whites in the message seemed to dispel the implicit concern that gains for non-white groups come at the expense of the white group.

Democrats have long sensed that mobilizing non-white communities risks alienating white voters. Ostfeld's research seems to confirm this risk. But the real danger to Democrats comes from reaching the wrong conclusions about what Ostfeld's work implies.

It's easy to imagine Democrats responding that, rather than risk alienating white voters, they should avoid efforts to mobilize the Latino community, or should do so only in narrowly targeted ways designed to ensure that as few whites as possible see ads that court Latino voters. Perhaps this might translate into supporting ads on Spanish-language media like Univision or Telemundo, but little more.

This conclusion almost certainly spells defeat for Democrats. Democrats have not won a majority of the white vote in a presidential election since 1964.[8] To defeat Trump, they need to win big among voters of color, including among those young people making this the most diverse rising generation ever. At the same time, though, Democrats must also build enthusiasm among white voters. Democrats cannot prevail if they choose one constituency over the other.

Nor do they need to make this self-defeating choice between mobilizing Latinos and building enthusiasm among whites. The research we conducted demonstrates that Democrats can use the same basic message—"because division is the main weapon against us, cross-racial solidarity is the best route forward for everyone"—to animate every racial group.

In our research, we tested various Democratic messages against a Republican message designed to trigger racial fear and resentment.[9] The Republican opposition message, in its entirety, read:

> Our leaders must prioritize keeping us safe and ensuring that hard working Americans have the freedom to prosper. Taking

a second look at people coming from terrorist countries who wish us harm or at people from places overrun with drugs and criminal gangs is just common sense. And so is curbing illegal immigration, so our communities are no longer flooded with people who refuse to follow our laws. We need to make sure we take care of our own people first, especially the people who politicians have cast aside for too long to cater to whatever special interest groups line their pockets, yell the loudest, or riot in the street.

Against this message, a progressive message stressing racial justice for communities of color did poorly. It seemed to reinforce, rather than challenge, the right's narrative that the country is locked into a zero-sum conflict between racial groups.

In contrast, a message promoting cross-racial solidarity to help all racial groups handily beat the right's message. Here's one version:

No matter where we come from or what our color, most of us work hard for our families. But today, certain politicians and their greedy lobbyists hurt everyone by handing kickbacks to the rich, defunding our schools, and threatening seniors with cuts to Medicare and Social Security. Then they turn around and point the finger for hard times at poor families, Black people, and new immigrants. We need to join together with people from all walks of life to fight for our future, just like we won better wages, safer workplaces, and civil rights in our past. By joining together, we can elect new leaders who work for all of us, not just the wealthy few.

Stripped to its essence, here's are the beats to the progressive message that consistently defeats narratives of racial fear: name shared values between racial groups; emphasize that the real threat comes from greedy elites who seek to divide us for their own ends; and call for groups to come together across racial lines to ensure society works all of us.

Messages aimed at mobilizing Latinos should parallel this form. The shared values might include *familia*, pride in moving for a better life, dignity, or myriad others. The threat comes from politicians and their billionaire backers who rig the system while seeking to divide us by demonizing Latino immigrants. And the call to action must clarify that building power for Latinos helps every racial group, whites included, because only a massive multi-racial progressive movement can get government back on the side of people rather than corporations.

My granddaughter gets it. When she marches in protests against the Trump administration, she jauntily waves a sign that promises "taco trucks on every corner."[10] Her placard is a smirky rejoinder to the head of Latinos for Trump, who in 2016 warned that, left unchecked, Hispanic culture would soon put "tacos trucks on every corner." Far from fearing this supposed infestation, resistors have instead elevated the coming taco truck bonanza into a tasty vision of a pluralistic future in which we all dine better.

Democrats should not retreat from mobilizing Latinos, African Americans, or other minority communities. But when reaching out to communities of color, liberals must take care to stress that empowering each group is good for every group—white, Black, and brown, natives to this continent and from across the globe. Let's guac the vote for all of us, of every color and hue.

Notes

1. A shorter version of this essay appeared in the *Los Angeles Times*, January 29, 2020.
2. Jens Manuel Krogstad, Ana Gonzalez-Barrera, and Christine Tamir. "Latino Democratic Voters Place High Importance on 2020 Presidential Election." *Pew Research Center* (blog). Accessed February 7, 2020. www.pewresearch.org/fact-tank/2020/01/17/latino-democratic-voters-place-high-importance-on-2020-presidential-election/.
3. Anthony Cilluffo, and Richard Fry. "An Early Look at the 2020 Electorate." *Pew Research Center's Social & Demographic Trends Project* (blog). Accessed February 7, 2020. www.pewsocialtrends.org/essay/an-early-look-at-the-2020-electorate/.
4. Luis Noe-Bustamante, and Antonio Flores. "Facts on Latinos in America." *Pew Research Center's Hispanic Trends Project* (blog). Accessed February 7, 2020. www.pewresearch.org/hispanic/fact-sheet/latinos-in-the-u-s-fact-sheet/.
5. Mara Cecilia Ostfeld. "The New White Flight? The Effects of Political Appeals to Latinos on White Democrats." *Political Behavior* 41, no. 3 (September 2019): 561–582. https://doi.org/10.1007/s11109-018-9462-8.
6. J. Baxter Oliphant. "6 Facts About Democrats in 2019." *Pew Research Center* (blog), June 26, 2019. www.pewresearch.org/fact-tank/2019/06/26/facts-about-democrats/.
7. Lake Research Partners, ASO Communications, and Brilliant Corners Research and Strategy. "Race Class Narrative: National Dial Survey Report." May 2018. www.ianhaneylopez.com/wp-content/uploads/2014/10/LRP-Report.Race-Class-Narrative.National-C4.pdf.

Latino Voter Outreach   89

8. Steve Phillips. "What About White Voters?" *Center for American Progress*, February 5, 2016. www.americanprogress.org/issues/race/news/2016/02/05/130647/what-about-white-voters/.
9. I discussed this research at length in a recent book. See Ian Haney López. *Merge Left: Fusing Race and Class, Winning Elections, and Saving America.* New York: The New Press, 2019.
10. Niraj Chokshi. "'Taco Trucks on Every Corner': Trump Supporter's Anti-Immigration Warning." *The New York Times*, September 2, 2016, sec. U.S. www.nytimes.com/2016/09/03/us/politics/taco-trucks-on-every-corner-trump-supporters-anti-immigration-warning.html.

18 Want More Black Voters? Meet Them Where They Live[1]

Karthik Balasubramanian

Black neighborhoods in key swing states hold enormous power to reshape politics in November 2020 and beyond. But in order to maximize this potential, progressives need to imagine and invest on an unprecedented scale.

Black voters have consistently supported Democratic candidates over Republicans by stunning margins: about 90% to 10%. No other major demographic comes close to this level of support—for either party.[2] For every 10 new black voters, nine will likely vote for a Democrat and one for a Republican, yielding eight net Democratic votes. In contrast, 10 new Latino voters (who voted 70% Democratic and 30% Republican in 2018) would produce four net Democratic votes. For white, college-educated women, the figure is two.

Said another way, one new black voter has the same net effect as two new Latino voters or four new white, college-educated female voters. While it is true that there are more eligible but nonvoting people of other important demographics, there are more net Democratic votes available from new black voters because of the huge differential in Democratic support.

What is a "new black voter"? In the 2016 presidential election, an estimated 3.3 million black people in six key swing states were unregistered, or registered but had never voted, or didn't vote in that year, despite previously doing so. In those six states (Michigan, Pennsylvania, Wisconsin, Florida, North Carolina, and Georgia) the number of eligible but nonvoting black people was at least 2.8 times Hillary Clinton's margin of loss. Five of these states also had Senate elections; Democrats lost all five.

In Pennsylvania,[3] for example, Mrs. Clinton lost by about 44,000 votes, while Katie McGinty, the Democratic Senate candidate, lost by about 87,000 votes. But an estimated 350,000 eligible black people didn't vote statewide. Combine this with the fact that half of

Meet Them Where They Live 91

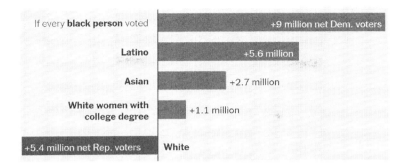

Figure 18.1 If Everyone Votes: Estimates of the additional net votes for Democrats and Republicans if everyone in these groups turned out in presidential elections. Full turnout by whites would result in a net gain for Republicans.

Source: The New York Times, analysis of 2018 exit polls and 2016 Voting and Registration Supplement to the Census Current Population Survey by Karthik Balasubramanian, Howard University; figures are rounded to nearest 100,000.

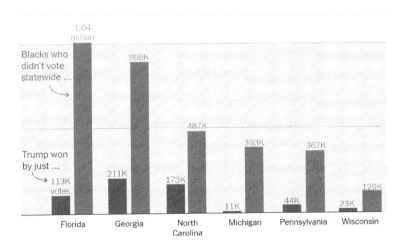

Figure 18.2 Six States That Matter: The number of blacks who didn't vote in 2016 far exceeded Donald Trump's winning margin in several key states.

Source: The New York Times, analysis of black citizen population estimates (2016 American Community Survey) and black citizen non-voting rates by state (2016 Voting and Registration Supplement to the Census Current Population Survey) by Karthik Balasubramanian, Howard University.

Pennsylvania's black population lives in Philadelphia, and it becomes clear where there is concentrated, untapped political power. This type of geographic concentration is not unique. Just 14 cities account for over half of the black population in these six crucial states. (In addition to the cities shown in Figure 18.2, there are also large concentrations of black nonvoters in Jacksonville, Tampa, and Orlando, Florida; and in Fayetteville and Winston-Salem, North Carolina.)

And within these 14 cities, majority-black census blocks (areas usually much smaller than election precincts) account for a vastly disproportionate percentage of the black population. For example, majority-black census blocks account for 80% of Milwaukee County's black population, which itself accounts for 70% of Wisconsin's black population. The upshot is clear: Nonvoting black residents in key places have the potential to swing elections, from the presidency on down, in 2020 and beyond. Republicans have understood these dynamics for years; they long ago decided that they were better off trying to suppress black voters than to compete for their votes.[4]

The argument here is not that Donald Trump's election in 2016 is the fault of black voters. Nobody but the 63 million Americans who voted for him bears responsibility for that. In fact, turnout patterns of black voters are largely similar to those of whites. Yes, it is true that black voters were slightly underrepresented in 2016 and slightly overrepresented in 2012. And in elections like the 2016 race with razor-thin margins, a small change in turnout can matter.

But by fixating on the small turnout differential from 2012 to 2016,[5] progressives miss the far larger prize: the more than 30% of all voters who consistently don't vote in presidential elections. In midterm and municipal elections, that figure is even higher. This is a result of progressives' failure to execute a plan ambitious enough to change the status quo.

How can we seize this opportunity? The political scientists Donald Green and Alan Gerber conducted an analysis of hundreds of voter turnout experiments that tested methods like yard signs, mailers, text messages, and TV ads.[6] No simple, inexpensive tactic improved turnout more than three percentage points on average in high-turnout elections. We've been answering the question: "Can we get a little by investing a little per targeted voter in the final three weeks before an election?" But we've never asked: "Can we get a lot by investing a lot far in advance of election season?"

Research shows that the most effective voter-turnout technique is person-to-person contact from a trusted source like a family member, friend, or neighbor; this is far more successful than impersonal paid communication like TV, digital, or radio ads. But most nonvoters or

Meet Them Where They Live   93

Trump won Wisconsin by **23,000 votes**		... but in Milwaukee, **93,000 blacks** didn't vote
Trump won Florida by **113,000 votes**		... but in Miami, **379,000 blacks** didn't vote
Trump won Michigan by **11,000 votes**		... but in Detroit, **277,000 blacks** didn't vote
Trump won Pennsylvania by **44,000 votes**		... but in Philadelphia, **238,000 blacks** didn't vote
Trump won North Carolina by **173,000 votes**		... but in Charlotte, Raleigh, Greensboro and Durham, **233,000 blacks** didn't vote
Trump won Georgia by **211,000 votes**		... but in Atlanta, **530,000 blacks** didn't vote

Figure 18.3 Big Cities, Big Voter Pools: Hillary Clinton came up short in several key states. But there were enough black voters in just a handful of cities that could have changed the outcome. (Cities represent metropolitan statistical areas.)

Source: *The New York Times,* analysis of black citizen population estimates (2016 American Community Survey) and black citizen non-voting rates by state (2016 Voting and Registration Supplement to the Census Current Population Survey) by Karthik Balasubramanian, Howard University.

infrequent voters don't get this kind of outreach because campaigns and independent political groups generally ignore people with low "turnout scores." And since these scores are developed based on voting history, nonvoters become less and less likely to be contacted. Even worse, people who have recently moved or are unregistered may not even show up in campaign databases. This problem is acute in areas with high transience, like urban, majority-black neighborhoods.

But the opportunity lies precisely with these people. To realize this potential, we must shed cynical assumptions about what is and isn't possible. Here is a proposal to develop a robust organizing infrastructure that can build real relationships with black nonvoters and maximize turnout.

In all the 14 cities, two residents in every micro-geography would be recruited, trained, and given a stipend to form a block team. The block team's first step would be to connect with a member of every household on the block—going back to every door as many times as necessary to make contact. This introductory interaction would be an unhurried conversation about the block team and its goals of building power and turnout, and it would gather the names of all voting-eligible people living at the residence. This data would then be reconciled with the voter file to categorize every eligible black resident by registration status and voting history. Let's say the block team has 100 black households with 200 eligible voters. Once the team gets good data, it can focus on deep canvassing—having meaningful conversations at the doorstep—with only the nonvoters or infrequent voters, maybe 80 people in all. In this conversation or future ones, block teams can help them register and make plans to vote, perhaps with a user-friendly tool like Map the Vote.[7]

This is not the only model or necessarily the best one, but it does typify the big thinking required to match the size of the opportunity. There are many questions that need to be answered: How many block teams can a full-time organizer train and support? How large an area can a block team effectively cover? How often should block teams meet? Should they focus on hyper-local, nonpartisan issues or on national partisan issues? We can't definitively answer these questions this year (maybe block teams should focus on 75 black households, instead of 100). But every year, there are two chances to continue refining the infrastructure. The 2021 municipal primary and general elections allow block teams to build on this year's lessons. When the 2022 elections for senators and governors are in full swing, block teams will have been able to refine their strategies even further.

The neighborhood team model is not new: Barack Obama's presidential campaigns empowered tens of thousands of ordinary people to achieve extraordinary levels of voter contact in their own neighborhoods.[8] But even the best-resourced political campaigns are hampered by a lack of time. They exist only for a few fleeting months every four years, often building infrastructure from scratch and leaving little behind for the next campaign.

So, who should build this permanent organizing infrastructure? Ideally, both state Democratic parties and independent political groups. State parties have a tremendous amount to gain: They could more effectively mobilize voters for priority issues cycle after cycle and have a vastly improved way to listen to marginalized voters and incorporate their ideas and frustrations into the party's platform. Independent groups can build community power apart from a political party, which could more easily hold elected officials accountable.

Some groups are already doing this. Black Leaders Organizing for Communities in Milwaukee,[9] for example, trains community ambassadors to turn their neighborhoods' resources into collective power that can be wielded to win. And Color of Change aims to do this on a national scale through its political arm called Voting While Black.[10] But such groups need an order of magnitude more funding, well before election season and on a regular basis, to seize this huge opportunity. Both the breadth and depth of their work are limited by insufficient and unpredictable investment. Genuine community organizing takes months and years, not days and weeks, a truth that is often lost on the donor community.

To be sure, big money on the Democratic side does exist—it's just not being spent effectively. A majority of the $1 billion that went toward Mrs. Clinton's candidacy was spent on paid communication like TV and digital ads—not on groups that could best facilitate neighbor-to-neighbor contact.

Enormous investment in organizing can build real power in traditionally marginalized neighborhoods and elect accountable politicians, now and for years to come. Done the right way, this will develop leaders and political power which can be used to achieve whatever people want—that's the true essence of democracy. We know black neighborhoods in six key states can get us there. Now we need to make it happen.

Notes

1. "Democrats Are Ignoring the Voters Who Could Decide This Election." By Karthik Balasubramaniam originally appeared in *The New York Times*, February 26, 2020.
2. Alec Tyson. "The 2018 Midterm Vote: Divisions by Race, Gender, Education." *Pew Research Center* (blog), November 8, 2018. www.pewresearch.org/fact-tank/2018/11/08/the-2018-midterm-vote-divisions-by-race-gender-education/.
3. "Pennsylvania Election Results 2016." *The New York Times*, September 13, 2017, sec. U.S. www.nytimes.com/elections/2016/results/pennsylvania.
4. Jamil Smith. "Exclusive: In Leaked Audio, Brian Kemp Expresses Concern Over Georgians Exercising Their Right to Vote." *Rolling Stone*, October 23, 2018. www.rollingstone.com/politics/politics-news/brian-kemp-leaked-audio-georgia-voting-745711/.
5. Bureau, US Census. "Voting in America: A Look at the 2016 Presidential Election." *The United States Census Bureau*. Accessed March 10, 2020. www.census.gov/newsroom/blogs/random-samplings/2017/05/voting_in_america.html.
6. Donald P. Green, and Alan S. Gerber. *Get Out the Vote: How to Increase Voter Turnout*, 4th ed. Washington, DC: Brookings Institution Press, 2019.
7. Map the Vote. "Map the Vote." Accessed March 10, 2020. https://mapthe.vote.
8. Joy Cushman. "Opinion | The Trump Campaign Knows Why Obama Won. Do Democrats?" *The New York Times*, August 26, 2019, sec. Opinion. www.nytimes.com/2019/08/26/opinion/republicans-obama-campaign-playbook.html.
9. BLOC. "BLOC." Accessed March 10, 2020. www.blocbybloc.org.
10. Color of Change. "Color of Change Helps You Do Something Real About Injustice." Accessed March 10, 2020. https://colorofchange.org; VotingWhileBlack. "Voting While Black." Accessed March 10, 2020. https://votingwhileblack.com/.

19 Winning Alabama, 2017
A Roadmap to Success?

Debra Cleaver

I've been a skeptic since birth, and I've been in this civic engagement game a long time now, meaning I've become something of an expert at challenging conventional electoral wisdom.

Conventional wisdom holds that voter registration is the key to increasing voter turnout, despite the fact that between 80 and 85% of Americans are already registered at any given point, yet no more than 65% have cast ballots over the past 100 or so years. If you trust self-reported census data, 90% of registered voters cast ballots. If you're like me, however, you've probably cross-referenced primary census data with U.S. Election Project turnout data and you've determined that approximately 30% of nonvoters are already registered to vote.[1] Which means if you want to increase voter turnout without breaking the bank, you should *focus on already registered voters* who might need a little bit of help to cast ballots.

Conventional wisdom also holds that low voter turnout is somehow due to voter apathy. This is utter nonsense: *voter turnout is low in the United States because it is objectively harder to cast a ballot* in the United States than in any other developed nation with democratically elected leadership. So, the next time you hear someone talking about "voter apathy," feel free to shout at them that they're echoing a conservative talking point which is designed to obscure decades of intentional voter suppression.

Conventional wisdom also tells us that the young people, people of color, and unmarried women who make up the New American Majority are all low-propensity voters (i.e., less likely to vote), and therefore we should not bother spending our outreach dollars on them. This is some grade-A racist, sexist, classist bullshit: *your voter propensity score is like a credit score, and it increases over time as you vote.* But many partisan groups use propensity scores to determine whom to engage and whom to ignore, and since they engage the high-propensity voters (older, wealthier, whiter voters) and ignore the rest, we find ourselves in a vicious and self-fulfilling cycle of neglected voters not casting ballots, which means they're likely to be neglected again (and not vote again) until the end result is an electorate which is disproportionately wealthy, white, married, and high income. Go figure.

Finally, conventional wisdom tells us that we can win elections by reaching across the aisle toward people who, quite literally, hate us. This is absurd. You're more likely to change your spouse than your political party and reaching across the aisle is an excellent way to guarantee that you'll spend a lot of money ignoring your base. There are only two ways to win elections in the United States. If you're a conservative, you win by decreasing turnout. *If you're a progressive, you win by increasing turnout.* That's it.

I'm going somewhere with all of this, I promise. For over a decade now I've been telling anyone who will listen that Americans want to vote and will vote in higher numbers and more consistently as voting becomes more convenient and accessible. And that we organizers need to spend less time "convincing" people to vote and *more time enabling people to vote by identifying and clearing roadblocks*. Sometimes these roadblocks are external, such as holding elections on a workday, and sometimes they're internal (such as simply not knowing when and where to go vote).

Which brings me to the Alabama Senate Special Election on December 12, 2017. Alabama is a special place, full of special racists, who have spent decades making it all but impossible for people of color (POC) to cast ballots. As a result, Alabama is a very red state, where the conventional wisdom holds that it is impossible for a Democrat to win. On top of that, Alabama does crazy things like hold Senate elections in December of an off-year, which is something you do when you want to all but guarantee low turnout. As a result, the conservative candidate wins, pretty much always. But that isn't what happened in December 2017, and I'm going to tell you why.

About six weeks before the election, a donor called me and asked if I thought a Democrat could win the Alabama Senate election. I immediately said yes. Here's why: a full 30% of the registered voters in Alabama are POC, and those voters are overwhelmingly Democrats; even the white voters cast Democratic ballots 18–23% of the time. Meanwhile, experts were predicting shockingly low turnout when compared to 2016 presidential turnout (60% in 2016 versus an anticipated 30% in 2017). So, if someone were to prevent POC voter attrition while letting white voter apathy just sort of happen, then yes, a

Democrat could, in theory, win in Alabama. It wouldn't be likely, but it was theoretically possible.

An important caveat: at the time of this conversation, I was running Vote.org, a nonpartisan organization I had founded in 2008 under the name Long Distance Voter. I'm a progressive human, but I always do nonpartisan work because I truly, deeply, believe that a rising tide lifts all boats, and that democracy only works when turnout is high. So, while elections themselves are partisan, and have partisan outcomes, I was mostly interested in seeing if I could blow a hole in the conventional wisdom about "low-propensity voters" and convert them into high-propensity voters by simply engaging them.

My proposition for my donor was simple, cost effective, and easy to launch. We would run a hyper-aggressive, multi-channel marketing campaign promoting the election itself via billboards, transit ads, peer-to-peer SMS, and direct mail (in partnership with the wonderful team at Voter Participation Center). *Our messaging would be simple*: Vote on Tuesday, December 12. We wouldn't mention candidates, but we would target majority POC census tracts. Two hours later I sent him a proposal. The entire project would cost $780,000 and target about 860,000 voters. In other words, it was cheap. My donor said he would do half if someone else would cover the other half. I found a match within 30 hours, and the project was a go.

There weren't any complicated data involved, and we didn't hire any strategists or advertising consultants. We used a company called Adquick *to buy every billboard and transit ad in a majority POC census tract*; we purchased cell phone numbers for registered POC from TargetSmart, a political data firm, and used the Hustle Peer-to-Peer SMS platform to message each person three or four times each; and we worked with Voter Participation Center to send two waves of mail to every household with a registered POC voter. Oh, and *we paid our texters, because we're progressive*, and there isn't anything cute or progressive about not paying people.

The billboards were nothing special, design-wise, but they were literally everywhere. They simply said "VOTE, Tuesday December 12." The billboards were so plain, in fact, that a friend of mine working out in Alabama said that she thought they were government billboards, given how boring the design was. It only took her a few seconds, of course, to realize that the state of Alabama was advertising an election where a Democrat had a good chance of winning.

We were in the middle of running this program when the Roy Moore scandal broke. In case you've forgotten, Roy Moore was credibly accused of pedophilia, which should have been disqualifying, but somehow wasn't. This is a man who had already been removed from the judicial branch twice, so the idea that he couldn't be beaten seemed ridiculous to me. I called my original donor and said, "Hey, this race is definitely competitive now," and continued running the program with one slight change. I updated the messaging on our peer-to-peer SMS messages to read that we were now expecting "record-high turnout." I was making this up, since I don't have a crystal ball, but I figured that it would *create some healthy social pressure*, or FOMO (fear of missing out), as the kids call it.

Meanwhile, the partisan experts from D.C. had decided I was batshit insane for believing that the Alabama Special Election was officially competitive. From what I could tell, none of the national Democratic groups were investing in the Doug Jones campaign, not even the DSCC, which exists solely to elect Democratic senators. The contrarian in me was pleased, while the American in me was pretty disappointed, if I'm being honest.

By now, you all know what happened. A record-setting high of 41% of the voting-eligible population cast ballots in the 2017 Alabama Special Senate Election. Democratic candidate Doug Jones defeated Republican candidate Roy Moore by a margin of 21,924 votes (1.7%), making Jones the first Democrat to win a U.S. Senate seat in Alabama since 1992. A key piece of the victory ended up being the higher than expected turnout among black voters. *Majority POC counties saw a turnout increase of 27% relative to the August primary, whereas majority-white counties saw an increase of just 16%.* And that, my friends, is what happens when you invest in "low-propensity" POC voters.

This election confirmed a lot of what I had suspected for years. First, *partisan groups spend a truly astonishing amount of money*, and they spend it poorly. Almost all of the $40–50 million spent by partisan groups in Alabama went to broadcast TV, despite the fact that 50% of people under 50 haven't seen a single minute of broadcast TV in over a year. Second, *you can't increase voter turnout without talking to people who have been deemed "less likely" to vote*. Third, *nonpartisan messaging works*, and you can increase turnout simply by reminding people that an election is coming. Not all candidates have Obama's charm, and partisan groups would be better served by promoting the idea of voting and agency of voting. Fourth, *if you increase turnout, you'll increase the diversity of the electorate*, and a diverse electorate is more likely to favor progressive candidates.

Finally, there is no election where the outcome is a foregone conclusion, and anyone who tells you otherwise is lying. If you assume the best of the voter, and simply clear roadblocks to voting, magical outcomes await.

Note

1. "Voter Turnout Data—United States Elections Project." Accessed March 30, 2020. www.electproject.org/home/voter-turnout/voter-turnout-data.

20 The Base Versus the Middle
A False Choice

Steve Israel

Students of election strategies, particularly the 2020 presidential campaigns, are drawn into a debate that seems to be fracturing the Democratic Party: should we prioritize voter turnout among progressive voters or persuasion among moderate swing voters? As former chairman of the Democratic Congressional Campaign Committee between 2011–2015, I don't believe that elections are won by offering the binary choice of turning out the base or appealing to swing voters. We have to do both.

First, let's understand the folly of any argument that marginalizes one segment of the electorate at a time when the survival of democratic norms is at stake. Defeating the Trump agenda will require a well-mobilized, inclusive, and collaborative effort. Like it or not, this will be a close election, and Democrats simply cannot afford to take a single vote or group of voters for granted. Every vote matters, not just some. A divided and chaotic Democratic Party is exactly what President Trump—and, I would add, Vladimir Putin—desire.

Second, let's understand where the presidential election will be won or lost. It's a formula I call 20/7/20.

Twenty percent of the likely electorate remains undecided about President Trump or his opponent. Eighty percent is intensely for or against him. Therefore, it is important to message to those undecideds, something true for Republicans as well as Democrats.

Seven states, at this point, will determine who wins or loses: Pennsylvania, Florida, North Carolina, Ohio, Wisconsin, Michigan, and Arizona. That's the strategic battleground.

About 20 swing counties in those seven states will determine who wins those states. For example, the key to winning Wisconsin is winning Kenosha County, outside of Milwaukee. President Obama and Vice President Biden won Kenosha (and Wisconsin) in 2008 and 2012. President Trump won the county and state in 2016.

The fact is that swing voters in those bellwether media markets tend to be fairly moderate. They want lower taxes, affordable and quality health care, and protections for women's health. Many also have 401(k) accounts, don't want to lose their private health insurance, and are wary of major economic disruptions. This doesn't mean that every voter in those places will only choose a moderate candidate, but a preponderance will.

But does a moderate candidate soften turnout among progressive voters? Is the conundrum best symbolized by a balance scale where adding moderates to one pan loses progressives on the other? If running on the far left loses moderates, and running on the moderate middle right loses the left, what is to be done?

The answer: exactly what the Democrats did in the spectacularly successful midterm elections when they won the House majority. They managed to appeal to both. They ran on progressive values (checking President Donald Trump, protecting pre-existing conditions in health care, acknowledging and addressing climate disruption), but also recruited and ran moderate candidates. And they gave those candidates the flexibility to message, mobilize, and organize without applying an ideological litmus test.

Here's an example: there's a Brooklyn in New York and a Brooklyn in Iowa. In New York, candidates must turnout the base with progressive vision and energy. But in Iowa, candidates must find support among moderate, swing voters. That is exactly what Rep. Abby Finkenauer did, and she flipped a Republican district. She turned out her base, pulled in swing voters, and won. She's one of the reasons Democrats won a majority and can check President Trump's abuses.

That playbook must be operative in 2020.

Finally, we have another task. According to the Knight Foundation, some 100 million eligible voters stayed home in 2016. Many felt disenfranchised, marginalized, neglected by both candidates. That represents a vast reservoir of votes for anti-Trumpists to cultivate. For those voters, it's not necessarily about left or right, it's about a candidate and a party that will move them forward and that identifies with the unique convergences that roil our economy. Don't neglect them.

Every campaign has two vital elements: turnout and persuasion. We must do both. We can continue a philosophical debate about whether the party brand is socialist, left of center, center, or right of center.

But how about winning this election first? Otherwise, our debates will be just that—strategic and ideological conversations empty of impact on the future of the country.

21 Unleashing Our Secret Weapon

Jeff Merkley

Stop me if you've heard this one before: Once there was a Philistine giant, an unbeatable warrior. A scrawny Israelite kid was the only one brave enough to take him on. . . . Ok, you know the rest.

There are a lot of days that a lot of us, We the People, feel like little David up against Goliath. The truth is, the privileged and powerful *have* rigged the economy. The ultrawealthy get richer and richer while folks in my blue-collar neighborhood work longer hours with fewer benefits and much higher expenses. They're barely hanging on.

And those powerful people *are* using that massive wealth to corrupt our democracy. Vast amounts of dark money swamp campaigns with attacks and lies. Politicians are designing convoluted districts to pick their voters, instead of voters picking their representatives, the way democracy is supposed to work. And voter suppression has roared back to strategically deny whole constituencies the chance to exercise the most fundamental right in a democracy: the right to vote.

It's a daunting battlefield we're looking at, as we stare across at this Goliath of big money and structural advantages. But never forget how that story ended: David won. And so can we.

Of course, David had a secret weapon: his slingshot. We have one too. If you look at the end of your wrist and close your hand, you'll see our secret weapon. We can overcome all of their advantages if we get out and knock on doors.

I know that grassroots passion and hard work is the most powerful force in politics, because I've seen it first-hand. When I first ran for state representative, I was a complete unknown. I had no money, no name recognition, no staff. What I had were flyers I printed off my home computer, a pair of sneakers, and a willingness to jog door to door, determined to get to every house in my district. My two opponents, both of whom had held office before, blanketed the major roads with their signs. My own friends kept asking me why they saw the other candidates' signs and never saw mine.

But while they were pounding in signs, I was pounding on doors. And it turned out, doors win. I would knock on a door, and find something to strike up a conversation about—a garden gnome, or the car in the driveway, or, my favorite, the family pooch. I'd ask them what was important to them. And I'd follow up later. I ended up winning half the vote.

Real democracy works. When people have a say in what our government does, they get involved.

That's why central to Donald Trump and Mitch McConnell's strategy for power is to beat us down, make us think we can't win. The fix is in, so why bother getting off the couch? A rigged system invites cynicism. Undermining faith in democracy works to their advantage.

But if we join together and unite behind the principles that our country was founded on, even if it has yet to realize them for all of its people, we can turn their cynical, anti-democratic, and anti-Democratic strategy against them.

The truth is, the Republican party can't win in a fair fight because their ideas are unpopular. Heck, their number one priority when they got control of the Congress and White House was taking health care away from tens of millions of people! They side with pharmaceutical companies instead of trying to bring down drug prices. They side with polluters instead of tackling the climate crisis that people see threatening their lives and livelihoods. They stop even the most rudimentary efforts to reduce gun violence despite overwhelming support. Republicans couldn't even make $1.5 trillion in tax cuts popular because, like most of their policies, they are trying to deliver more wealth and power to the wealthy and powerful.

The less popular Republicans get, the more they treat government by and for the people like a threat. That's why they try to stop people from voting, or gerrymander districts so their votes count less. It's why they're beholden to massive dark money spending to attack their opponents and avoid a real debate on the issues. Instead of trying to convince a majority of *all* Americans to support them, Republicans are now committed to a strategy of stoking their shrinking base with fear and preventing and discouraging others from voting.

So the gap keeps growing between what people want and what a minority government increasingly of, by, and for the powerful gives them. That disconnect between aspiration and reality can fuel cynicism, but it can also fuel change. The pressure to address the real problems people face keeps building, and our task is to unleash it in a massive blue wave in 2020 that sweeps away the anti-democratic obstacles Republicans have built up.

We absolutely can do this. Donald Trump is president because he won Wisconsin, Michigan, and Pennsylvania by a combined total of 80,000 votes. That number is dwarfed by the 4.4 million 2012 Obama voters across America who didn't vote in 2016. We have the numbers to win. And if we win, we are ready to transform America so our government actually works for the people.

When Democrats flipped the House in 2018, the very first thing they did was put forward the most comprehensive anti-corruption, pro-democracy package in decades. The For the People Act, H.R.1, would register tens of millions of new voters.[1] It would put grassroots, small donors in charge instead of wealthy contributors. It would end partisan gerrymandering and address some of the biggest ethical breaches of this presidency.

The House passed it, and every Democratic senator cosponsored it when Tom Udall and I brought it to the Senate. When we take the White House and the Senate, and keep the House, the first order of business will be passing the For the People Act. It's the key to changing how government works and whom it works for.

If we do that, there is a pathway to do so many of the things that people want but that have been thwarted by the government serving the powerful. There's no magic wand, and we won't solve all of our problems once and for all. But if we break the death grip the privileged and powerful have on the government, we can make progress in bringing down drug prices, pass LGBTQ protections, strengthen labor unions, invest in infrastructure, make child care more affordable, address the housing crisis, and so much more.

It all starts with unleashing that secret weapon. If we mobilize a grassroots army, we can make America what it is supposed to be: a place that offers opportunity and justice to everyone, no matter the color of their skin, their gender, the language they speak, or what side of the railroad tracks they live on. Government of, by, and for the people is both our birthright and our responsibility. Let's go get it.

Note

1. John P. Sarbanes. "H.R.1–116th Congress (2019–2020): For the People Act of 2019 (2019)." www.congress.gov/bill/116th-congress/house-bill/1.

22 Voting Ourselves a Raise

Saru Jayaraman

We have been ignoring one of the largest and fastest growing electorates in the United States at our peril.

I happened to live and work in New York City on 9/11, when among many other thousands, 73 workers in the restaurant at the top of the World Trade Center called 'Windows on the World' lost their lives. I was asked to help co-found a relief center in the aftermath of the tragedy, both for the families of the victims and for the 13,000 restaurant workers who lost their jobs in the aftermath. What started as a relief center grew into a national organization of restaurant workers, employers, and consumers organizing for better wages and working conditions in the nation's food service sector.

In 2013, our research and experiences with low-wage workers led us to focus our efforts on the subminimum wage for tipped workers in particular. There are 13 million restaurant workers and nearly 6 million tipped workers across the United States, including restaurant, car wash, nail salon, tech platform delivery, and other workers. The restaurant industry is both the largest segment of tipped workers and the second largest and absolute fastest growing sector of the U.S. economy overall, but it is also the lowest paying.[1] The National Restaurant Association (the other NRA) has argued since Emancipation that, given customer tips, businesses should be able to pay their tipped employees a subminimum wage, today just $2.13 an hour federally. A legacy of slavery, the subminimum wage for tipped workers today is a gender equity issue; 70% of tipped workers are women, disproportionately women of color, who work in nail and hair salons and casual restaurants like IHOP and Denny's, live in poverty at three times the rate of the rest of the U.S. workforce, and suffer from the worst sexual harassment of any industry because they are forced to tolerate inappropriate customer behavior in order to feed their families in tips.[2]

Seven states—California, Oregon, Washington, Alaska, Minnesota, Nevada, and Montana—have rejected this legacy of slavery and have eliminated the lower wage for tipped workers. Our research shows that these seven states have comparable or higher restaurant sales per capita, comparable or higher job growth among tipped workers and the restaurant industry overall, comparable or higher tipping averages than the 43 states with lower wages for tipped workers, and *half the rate of sexual harassment in the restaurant industry*.[3] One in two young women in America work in restaurants as their first job and learn what is acceptable in the workplace by subjecting themselves to objectification to earn their income in tips. The two-tiered wage system in restaurants thus sets the standard for a woman's worth economy-wide. And the problem has unfortunately expanded as the subminimum wage for tipped workers and the concept of tips as wage replacement has expanded to other low-wage workers—nail salon workers, car wash workers, parking and airport valets, and now even app-based delivery workers and drivers.

In a survey we conducted with more than 10,000 restaurant workers nationwide, we found that in region after region, workers overwhelmingly named their abysmally low wages, and in particular the subminimum wage for tipped workers, as their highest priority concern. In December 2019 we worked with Lake Research Associates to again conduct polling of tipped workers broadly in Massachusetts, Pennsylvania, New York, and Mississippi, and found that an overwhelming majority of tipped workers in each of these states reported that One Fair Wage would be an issue that would motivate them to vote.

Based on learning this information from workers, in 2013, we launched the campaign for One Fair Wage—calling on all states and the federal government to follow the lead of the seven states and require all employers to pay a full minimum wage with tips on top. As we began to organize workers for One Fair Wage in various states—and actually won One Fair Wage in Maine, Washington, D.C., and Michigan—we continually faced the overwhelming opposition of the National Restaurant Association, one of the most powerful and well-funded lobbies in Congress and state legislatures nationwide. With every minimum wage increase in the 43 states, legislators—most often Democrats—would reach a compromise with the "Other NRA" to leave tipped restaurant workers out of minimum wage increases. This was the same compromise that Democrats had struck with the NRA again and again over the last 81 years in 43 states and at the federal level—in order to raise the minimum wage, leave and leave these women out.

The result? An immense population of workers—13 million workers, in fact one of the nation's largest and fastest growing workforces—largely women, who are struggling with both severe economic insecurity and daily harassment, and who as a result are largely disconnected and distrustful of the political process and everyone connected with it. They are the epitome of the Rising American Electorate—as women, disproportionately women of color, disproportionately younger, single, especially single mothers—who largely have not voted. As low-wage workers who stand to benefit from many of the policies the Democratic Party purportedly espouses, they might be prime candidates for Democratic-leaning voters, but the disengagement is mutual: the Democratic Party has largely ignored them as "unlikely voters," and these workers largely do not vote and do not trust the Democratic Party. After all, they have seen Democratic elected officials throw them under the bus every time the minimum wage has increased.

After several years of both polling workers on the issues they care about most and observing these workers actually turnout to vote when One Fair Wage was on their ballot, we sounded the alarm. In 2016, we reached out to Secretary Clinton's campaign team with a message: we are sitting on a goldmine of over 13 million workers who largely do not vote, and we know the issue that will get them to the polls. Work with us, we said, to reach them. They will turn out to vote themselves a raise, and to vote for candidates who campaign on delivering One Fair Wage. Unfortunately, the campaign team was unconvinced.

After the devastation of the November 2016 election, we set out to prove what we believed the Party had missed, particularly in key states that should not have been lost, like Michigan. In 2017, the One Fair Wage campaign collected 400,000 signatures to put a One Fair Wage ballot measure on the Michigan ballot in November 2018. The ballot measure would raise the minimum wage for all workers to $12 an hour, and in particular would raise the subminimum wage for tipped workers from its current paltry rate of $3.52 an hour to $12 an hour over several years. Terrified that it would motivate Democratic-leaning voters to the polls, the Republican-controlled Michigan state legislature adopted our ballot measure as law—tripling wages for tipped workers in the state. But in doing so, they publicly declared that they were passing One Fair Wage simply to keep working people from going to vote and promised to gut the bill after the election.

We thus partnered with the Analyst Institute to run a state-wide relational voter program (RVP) using this issue to motivate unlikely restaurant and other low-wage worker voters through peer-to-peer voter engagement in both urban and rural parts of Michigan. In particular, we hired organizers, not canvassers, in different parts of the state to conduct outreach in restaurant-heavy districts in order to identify and develop nearly 5,000 low-wage worker leaders who each put about 10 of their peers' contacts in the restaurant industry into an app called My RVP List, which then helped them easily contact their peers multiple times leading up to the election, with the message "We just won a raise. If we want to keep it, we have to go vote out the people who are going to take it away." In this way, our 5,000 worker leaders produced a universe of over 20,000 restaurant and other low-wage worker voters who were encouraged by their peers to vote on the issue that matters to them most. We also ran a canvass with an additional 80,000 workers, using the same message.

Our relational voter program resulted in a 200–300% voter increase among restaurant workers from 2014 to 2018. The Analyst Institute's evaluation of the program showed that it was highly impactful, even controlling for other factors leading to higher voter engagement in 2018.

We learned three things from this experience. First, it is most effective to organize restaurant and other low-wage workers to vote based on the issue that matters most to them—their wages. Particularly for tipped workers, who had not seen any increases for decades, even when other workers' wages went up, voting out candidates who would stop their raises and being able to support candidates who commit to standing up to the likes of the National Restaurant Association and passing One Fair Wage was a huge motivator for these workers to vote, often for the first time.

Second, the peer-to-peer voter engagement methodology, modeled after the organizing principles that we had long used as a worker organizing group, is most effective with low-wage workers, especially in the restaurant industry. Restaurant workers work together in team environments; they live together, socialize together, even date one another, and are highly socially networked online. They are far more likely to trust their peers in their industry than any candidate or canvasser. If their peers tell them that there is a real pathway to wage increases, and it involves voting, there can be no better motivator to vote.

Third, having organized workers in this way to vote, it is imperative to continue to organize these workers to win raises and the changes they need to improve their lives. In our case, after the election we worked to recruit the workers in our RVP program as permanent members of our organization, and then to develop them as leaders mobilizing to demand One Fair Wage. After the November 2018 election, the Republican-controlled Michigan legislature did in fact reverse One Fair Wage, reducing workers' wages from going up to $12 back down to $3.52 an hour. We mobilized hundreds by reaching out to the workers who had been part of the RVP program, and worked with the newly-elected governor and attorney general—Democrats for the first time in 50 years, in part due to our efforts—to sue the legislature for attempting to adopt and amend a ballot measure in the same legislative session. The Michigan Supreme Court punted on the issue, leaving the new attorney general the power to declare the legislature's actions unconstitutional and thus make One Fair Wage the law in Michigan.

For too long, the Democratic Party machine has focused on voting as the endgame, as the only outcome worth measuring. When a low-wage worker votes but then sees an elected official they voted for fail to deliver—including failing to raise wages—they become disillusioned. Turning out to vote cannot simply result in a changed political regime—it must result in real changes to people's lives, or that turnout will likely never happen again.

For 2020, we are replicating the Relational Voter Program in Michigan, once again, and also in Pennsylvania, where Governor Tom Wolf and Democrats in the Republican-controlled legislature have championed a One Fair Wage bill that they have committed to pass if they gain control of the legislature. We will be mobilizing over 110,000 low-wage worker voters in these two states using the RVP. As we have widened our campaign to include new growing sectors of tipped workers beyond the restaurant industry, including car wash workers, nail salon workers, massage therapists and other care workers, and—perhaps the fastest growing sector—tech-platform delivery workers, we have the potential to be able to reach a wider audience of low-wage workers in rural parts of these states who are all affected by and can be motivated by One Fair Wage. Pennsylvania and Michigan are both battleground states for the presidential election and thus our program will help to prove the point we tried to make to the Democratic Party in 2016—that this immense and growing electorate can turnout for Democrats *if* elected officials commit to raising their wages over the lobbying of the NRA, and *if* they are organized by their peers to turnout on this issue, and then engaged after the election to actually win the issue.

This kind of relational voter program with low-wage worker sectors focused on the issues that matter to them most can be replicated in 2020 and beyond to motivate all 13 million restaurant workers in all 50 states to vote—but also to motivate low-wage workers in other sectors. Focusing on key issues like the minimum wage, developing leaders who can reach out to their peers based on the principles of community and worker organizing, and continuing to organize these leaders and members after the election to actually win the changes they sought in voting are all tactics that can be used effectively in any state and in any low-wage worker sector.

Without this kind of effort, however, our democracy is doomed. With economic inequality at its highest rates in our nation's history, low-wage sectors are no longer at the margin—they are the largest and fastest growing sectors of the United States economy. And low-wage workers in America largely do not vote. Without focus on actually delivering real policy change like raising wages for these sectors, there will be no way to engage these immense and growing sectors politically—no way to build the political will we need to win on climate change, reproductive justice, health care, or anything else. Using One Fair Wage and other wage issues as a motivator to vote is not simply about turnout; if we do not actually raise these workers' wages, so low that these workers are forced to work two and three jobs, they will never have the time, resources, and capacity to engage politically on any other issue. On the other hand, if we invest in long-term organizing—and voter engagement based on organizing—to win real changes in these workers' lives, we have the opportunity to engage tens of millions of new voters to win lasting political change.

Notes

1. Bureau of Labor Statistics. "Occupational Employment Statistics, 2011–2015." Accessed August 12, 2016. www.bls.gov/oes/tables.htm.
2. Restaurant Opportunities Centers United, Family Values @ Work, et al., "Tipped Over the Edge: Gender Inequity in the Restaurant Industry." February 2012. http://rocunited.org/wp-content/uploads/2012/02/ROC_GenderInequity_F1-1.pdf. While only 7% of American women work in the restaurant industry, more than a third (37%) of all sexual harassment claims to the Equal Employment Opportunity Commission come from the restaurant industry. See: E. Tahmincioglu. "Sexual Claims Common in Pressure-Cooker Restaurant World." November 1, 2011. Accessed September 13, 2014. http://business.nbcnews.com/_news/2011/11/01/8565198-sexualclaims-common-in-pressure-cooker-restaurant-world.
3. Bureau of Labor Statistics. "Quarterly Census of Employment and Wages 2015." Accessed August 9, 2016. www.bls.gov/cew/; Bureau of Labor Statistics. "2012 Economic Census." Accessed August 9, 2016. www.census.gov/econ/.

23 Moms for Housing
Inspiring the Movement for Housing as a Human Right

Nikki Fortunato Bas

On January 14, 2020, at 5 a.m.,[1] the Alameda County Sheriff's Office arrived at 2928 Magnolia Street in West Oakland, California, in riot gear with automatic rifles and armored vehicles to evict the homeless mothers who had been occupying the house. It was a heavily militarized operation that rattled elected officials who had previously remained silent about Moms for Housing.

I proudly stood with Moms4Housing before the eviction[2]—the only elected official to personally join them at their home and in court, drawing heat from many who disagreed with the moms' actions. To me, the moms were following the tradition of Dr. Martin Luther King, Jr., who taught us that sometimes breaking an unjust law is the right thing to do. The moms were engaging in an act of civil disobedience[3] to bring attention to the civil rights issue of our time: housing is a human right.[4]

So many people in Oakland and nation-wide don't have basic shelter. Our laws, systems, and markets—broken and inadequate—are stacked against our most vulnerable neighbors, making it incredibly difficult for them to obtain adequate shelter and provide stability and safety for themselves and loved ones.

I do not support anyone breaking into another's home. The moms chose this home because it had been vacant in their neighborhood for two years and was owned by a corporate real estate speculator. They took a path of nonviolent civil disobedience to shelter their children and call attention to a system that continues to leave working families and homeless individuals behind.

Throughout history, what is just, moral, and humane has not always aligned with the law. That is why our legislatures at every level are constantly reviewing, revising, and writing new laws. It was once legal to redline[5] Black communities and families, preventing them from accessing mortgage loans to buy homes, creating a lasting racial home-ownership gap.

These brave mothers have sparked a movement,[6] revealing corporate speculators who profit off of the housing crisis by leaving homes vacant for years. Investors nationwide are purchasing homes at rates higher than ever before;[7] they have bought one in five homes in the bottom third price range, taking away units from first-time, lower-income home buyers.

These moms are on the front lines, changing the dialogue about homelessness, capitalism, morality, and justice, to address the housing affordability and homelessness crises that impact us all. I stand with them because throughout our nation's history, civil disobedience has raised moral issues and built movements to make our laws more humane.

Looking back at this in the future, we will see a critical moment where communities came together to meet the immediate needs of the everyday people most impacted by injustice.

Housing is not a commodity to be bought and sold to maximize profits. We must hold accountable corporate speculators like Wedgewood, who owns the Magnolia Street property, who drive up housing costs, displacement, and homelessness, profiting off the foreclosure crisis. Learn more[8] about Wedgewood's massive real estate portfolio, home-flipping practices, and the more than 300 lawsuits that have occurred primarily over their attempts to evict tenants.

We must see the big picture that informs the moms' civil disobedience and call to action: While the house sat vacant for two years, homelessness in Oakland increased by 47%. At the current rental market rate, one must earn at least $40 an hour to afford a two-bedroom apartment.[9] These rents are simply out of reach for working-class families and individuals. The homes across the street from Mom's House are selling for $1.5 million on average.

We must also pause and celebrate our movement's victories. On January 20, 2020, Wedgewood agreed to negotiate the sale[10] of the Mom's House with the Oakland Community Land Trust.

These moms have inspired people across the entire country, and they are giving elected officials the moral courage to finally treat housing as a human right.

I am continuing to support and work with Moms4Housing. In Oakland the Moms for Housing Tenant Opportunity to Purchase and Community Ownership Act, if passed, will create:

- The first opportunity for tenants to purchase their homes when the owner decides to sell (tenants make up 60% of Oaklanders), and

- More "community ownership" by creating an opportunity for nonprofit housing developers, community land trusts, and the City to acquire vacant, investor-owned properties, prioritizing them to shelter people rather than for flipping-for-cash schemes. There are at least 6,000 vacant homes in Oakland, which is more than enough to house Oakland's 4,000 unhoused residents.

Our movement is just beginning; please join us!

What You Can Do:

1. Across the nation, vote for candidates who believe that *housing is a human right*.
2. Stay updated and get involved with the housing movement nationally. In Oakland, support my office's efforts to increase deeply affordable housing and to get investor-owned and abandoned homes into the community, and advocate for the same with your elected officials.[11]
3. Support taking homes off the speculative market and make them permanently affordable. With Oakland's $12 million Permanent Affordability Fund,[12] which my office created, tenants are assisted in purchasing their homes with land trusts and co-ops. If you are a property owner or know neighbors at risk of being displaced due to their building's imminent sale, a partnership with a Land Trust can save tenants from losing their homes, preserve the building for permanent affordability, and promote community ownership. Nationally, since 2007, the Right to the City Alliance has promoted these solutions through its dozens of local affiliates.[13] Similarly, in the November elections, candidates advocating these solutions, as opposed to Trump's and the Republican's corporate agenda, deserve our support.

Notes

1. Marisa Kendall. "Moms 4 Housing Members Arrested, but They're Not Going Away." *East Bay Times*, January 15, 2020. www.eastbaytimes.com/2020/01/14/moms-4-housing-members-arrested-but-theyre-not-going-away/.
2. "Moms 4 Housing." *Moms 4 Housing*. http://moms4housing.org/.
3. Molly Solomon. "'We're Not Leaving': Homeless Mom Says After Judge Orders Oakland Home Vacated." *KQED*, January 10, 1970. www.kqed.org/news/11795419/judge-orders-homeless-mothers-to-leave-oakland-home.

4. Ericka Cruz Guevarra, and Molly Solomon. "The Moral Case Behind 'Housing Is a Human Right'." *KQED*, January 3, 1970. www.kqed.org/news/11793704/west-oakland-housing-human-right-moms4housing.
5. Tracy Jan. "Redlining Was Banned 50 Years Ago: It's Still Hurting Minorities Today." *The Washington Post*. WP Company, March 28, 2018. www.washingtonpost.com/news/wonk/wp/2018/03/28/redlining-was-banned-50-years-ago-its-still-hurting-minorities-today/.
6. ACCE Action. "Today, the Courts Ruled in Favor of..." *Facebook Watch*, 2020. www.facebook.com/CalOrganize/videos/374264596778267/.
7. Laura Kusisto. "Investors Are Buying More of the U.S. Housing Market Than Ever Before." *The Wall Street Journal*. Dow Jones & Company, June 20, 2019. www.wsj.com/articles/investors-are-buying-more-of-the-u-s-housing-market-than-ever-before-11561023120.
8. Michael Bott, and Sean Myers. "Examining Wedgewood: A Look at the Home-Flipping Giant in Battle with Homeless Mothers." *NBC Bay Area*, January 6, 2020. www.nbcbayarea.com/investigations/examining-wedgewood-a-look-at-the-home-flipping-giant-in-battle-with-homeless-mothers/2208119/.
9. Marisa Endicott. "The Rent in the Bay Area Is Too Damn High. So These Moms Occupied a Vacant House." *Mother Jones*, January 7, 2020. www.motherjones.com/politics/2019/12/bay-area-moms-homeless-squatters/?fbclid=IwAR3UzQpO8TTcssKo3DBvHr1EpxJ_mpdeuinmufKxGCiv3PGZW5L1RdQYOfU.
10. Sarah Ravani. "Moms 4 Housing: Deal Reached to Negotiate Sale of West Oakland House to Nonprofit." *SFChronicle.com*, January 21, 2020. www.sfchronicle.com/bayarea/article/Deal-reached-to-sell-homeless-mothers-West-14989721.php.
11. Niki Fortunato Bas. "Sign Up for District 2 Councilmember Nikki Fortunato Bas' Newsletter." *Google*. Accessed March 6, 2020. https://docs.google.com/forms/d/e/1FAIpQLSfEBqc3J37cbRl_bTRqt68erFvdK1UmoFNyjBP2DVs-7Ps3sQ/viewform.
12. "Oakland's Bold Investment to Address Displacement & Promote Community..." *City of Oakland*. Accessed March 6, 2020. www.oaklandca.gov/news/2019/op-ed-oaklands-bold-investment-to-address-displacement.
13. Right to the City Alliance. "Right To The City Alliance." Accessed March 17, 2020. https://righttothecity.org.

24 Public Schools and the Path to a Political Majority

Helen Gym

In a political moment of extreme cynicism and despair, every election is a chance to reset our political climate and change the way we take power through our vote.

I grew up in an immigrant family, worked for more than two decades as a community organizer in immigrant rights and public education, and today I'm leading a movement-based agenda as a city councilmember in Philadelphia. I've thought long and hard about how political moments like this relate to the movements we've built for justice.

The odds are against us.

Even in a city like mine that is 7–1 registered Democrat, almost a half million voters routinely avoid the polling booth on major elections. In Pennsylvania, 40% of voters decided to stay home in November 2016. I knew that as a woman of color working in a city that is demographically and politically so different from the rest of the state, *how* we talk and work together on an issue like schools was as important as *what* we were talking about in any given moment.

Public schools allowed us to ground our politics in an issue that resonated all across the state.

Pennsylvania ranks 50th—the worst in the nation—when it comes to the funding gap between the poorest and wealthiest school districts.[1] You don't need a statistic to know what that inequality means to a child. For us in Philadelphia, it means we have to fight to get lead out of our drinking water and asbestos out of our schools. It means our kids are guaranteed a metal detector, security guards, and surveillance cameras before they get a music and art teacher, sufficient counselors, and a school librarian. It means our kids start school weeks later than students in better-funded school districts because we can't afford to air condition sweltering classrooms in August.

It means that the cynical and corporate-driven politics of both parties have failed us. A GOP-controlled state legislature had taken over my school district in 2002, dismantled our local school board, and scapegoated teachers. Meanwhile, Democrats were also complicit in peddling sham theories of privatization, high-stakes testing, and budget cuts.

With this kind of opposition, our work began locally, in schoolyards and backyard BBQs, at parent meetings and in places of worship—places where parents, youth, and teachers could have a voice. This is where we could talk through not only our outrage and frustrations, but our resilience and hope—where we could find new leaders and build for a larger mandate for public equity and justice. While this movement began in the streets, it soon moved into our board of education and city hall, and folks started paying attention. Not just in Philadelphia, but around the state and across the nation.

By 2014, the coalition that rose up around the fight for our public schools was unlike any that had been seen before—it united so many threads of my city's social justice fabric. Labor brought not just teachers and principals to the streets, but building engineers, maintenance workers, nurses, and bus drivers. Members of the clergy, social workers, and public health advocates followed suit. They not only joined parents, grandparents, and caretakers—they often were the parents, grandparents, and caretakers of our students.

As our coalition broadened, the stakes got higher. In 2011, a Republican governor cut $1 billion from the state education budget, resulting in school closings, higher taxes, and a slash and burn approach to essential school programs all over Pennsylvania. This was no longer a Philadelphia issue; it was now a statewide campaign to retake our schools, reform our electoral map, and set organizing as the foundation for democratic change.

We took our organizing work from the streets straight to electoral politics. We were already effective in working with community groups to knock doors, make phone calls, and run a media strategy to defend our public schools. From press conferences to rallies to call-in talk shows to opinion pieces in the mainstream press, we were training ourselves to make public schools a central talking point in everyday conversation.

This time, though, with so much at stake, we worked with our labor unions—particularly teachers and maintenance and service workers—to learn how to convert community based organizing techniques into electoral strategies. Now our door knocking and phone banking were broader and more targeted toward taking on our governor.

The Path to a Political Majority 119

In the fall of 2014, when state after state fell to the GOP in the midterms, Pennsylvania made history by becoming the only state in the nation to go red to blue. Yes, we threw out that governor who was the face of school budget cuts (making him the first one-term governor in Pennsylvania history) and elected a governor who ran on public school investments.

The following year, we sent corporate reformers packing and elected a mayor and city council—including myself—in a local election where universal access to quality public schools was the number-one voter issue. We also flipped our state supreme court with three new justices who came out of the strongholds of the public education battles in the state—Philadelphia and Allegheny County (Pittsburgh).

So, what did it mean for an education movement to take office? Did we prove unable to govern?

It turns out, we became one of the most effective political and social forces in the city in a generation.

Not only did we end a near two-decade state takeover of our public schools and install a local school board for the first time in a generation, we restored nurses, counselors, social workers, music programs, and clean water to every student in our public schools—proving that local leadership meant local victories.

- Our state supreme court has since ruled to end federal gerrymandering and this summer they'll hold a trial on the constitutionality of Pennsylvania's school funding formula.[2,3]
- We took on poverty and corporate power and passed the country's strongest Fair Workweek law, establishing the right to stable schedules for more than 130,000 low-wage workers.[4]
- We've ensured for the first time that renters facing eviction have a right to free legal counsel.[5]
- We're ending cash bail, and we've reduced mass incarceration so much that we closed down a county prison in just two years.[6]
- We disempowered ICE by ending municipal sharing agreements and fighting family detention.[7]

The 2018 and 2019 elections saw suburban regions around Philadelphia go blue, many for the first time in history and with education as a central issue.[8] Here at home, Philadelphians re-elected me with the highest vote count of any councilmember in decades.[9] They also elected the first third-party candidate in history to city council—a single mom who had worked with me on the school privatization battles just a few years earlier.[10]

And turnout was up by 25%. Fifty-thousand more Philadelphia voters pulled a lever for education and a broader justice movement in November 2019 than four years earlier.

None of this was by accident. Our fight for public education was just the starting point for something larger—a recognition that, in the same ways that we came together to uplift student and parent voices and reclaim our schools, we also could unite to take on profit-obsessed, regressive powers that doubled down on gerrymandering, on private prisons, on fracking, and on corporate welfare.

And by building and investing in a real, public-education movement, we were building the future political majority that within five years had remade the political map for one of the most hotly contested states in the nation.

What do these community and political victories of the last decade mean for Get Out the Vote (GOTV) in battleground states in 2020 and beyond?

Public education resonates in every state and especially in states that the Democratic party has lost over the decades. Look at the success of statewide teacher strikes in Oklahoma, West Virginia, Arizona, and Kentucky. Fair pay for teachers kickstarts conversations about wealth inequality, the gender wage gap, and the state of our middle class.

When Pennsylvania, Wisconsin, Ohio, and Texas moved to limit collective bargaining, slash benefits and pay, and scapegoat teachers, public school educators became a highly mobilized political force for the importance of unions and expanding labor protections in local elections. As we work to GOTV in communities that are often tuned out of and turned off from political candidates, public school teachers, counselors, nurses, and educators can become crucially important GOTV partners.

What we found was that when it came to our public schools, voters didn't hew to any particular ideology. When people see a neighborhood school close down because of budget cuts, when they lose a school nurse or they watch class sizes balloon higher, they get radical really fast.

When an issue is seen as a crisis in which their own children's lives are at stake, voters care less about what end of the ideological spectrum we're on than whether we're protecting and offering real solutions for their children. When we involved teachers, nurses, librarians, and school counselors at the door, voters moved even closer toward us.

The Path to a Political Majority   121

All but a handful of states in the nation have charter schools, one of the most divisive issues around public education. While charter schools were initially conceptualized as laboratories of innovative teaching and learning, they were quickly co-opted by privatizers, profiteers, and charlatans who ignored underlying issues of underfunding and poverty and instead blamed teachers and families while driving disinvestment from public schools.

In states like Michigan, Pennsylvania, and Florida, the charter laws are among the worst in the country—allowing for gross overspending on privately managed schools that have far too little oversight or are run by for-profit entities. Charter schools embody the concept of privatization in public education and the unfair and unjust funding of a few students over the needs of the majority of American children who attend public schools.

While Bush- and Obama-era policies allowed charter schools to proliferate, Donald Trump and his Education Secretary, Betsy DeVos, are fronting a "Department of Mis-Education." They have cut billions out of the federal education budget and used taxpayer dollars to expand failed privatization measures from for-profit schools to student debt exploiters to vouchers. Their "school choice" agenda does nothing for the majority of American children, attacks teachers and educators, and aims to dismantle public education as we know it. This is not an issue that comes out of D.C. think tanks; this is a bread-and-butter issue at the door of many taxpayers and American families.

One of the hardest conversations for progressives to face at the door are taxes. But taxpayers and voters are remarkably responsive to big investments and especially investments in children. Higher school taxes are a reflection of reduced state investment, especially in rural and underfunded communities. Demanding greater investment in our schools is a vehicle to talk about progressive taxation and meaningful investments that contrast with corporate tax cuts and pork-barrel boondoggles.

When a president exploits racial division and xenophobic hate, talking about schools as homes for immigrant youth, special-needs young people, and the diaspora and diversity of children who are our neighbors and our collective responsibility can be a crucial counter to the politics of hate.

Few things illustrate gross inequity more than the difference between a modern school building in a wealthy neighborhood and a crumbling school in an underfunded school district. Use the fact that most schools are polling locations to drive home the close connection between public education and reinvestment. Our school buildings are a means to build, modernize, and invest in every neighborhood—not just downtowns, ports, and business centers. When we build schools, we create jobs and build the cities and towns of our future.

No matter what you choose to talk about, in every election, our movement must come to the ballot box with a mandate for equity and for transformative change.

When we hit the streets, knock doors, and engage in real and meaningful conversations, this political moment becomes about more than one candidate or one issue. It becomes about us. It becomes about a collective vision for how we transform from strangers and passersby into climate activists, public education champions, and criminal justice reformers.

Believing in something matters. Caring matters. Our lives—not just politics—matter.

Notes

1. Emma Brown. "Pa. Schools Are the Nation's Most Inequitable: The New Governor Wants to Fix That." *Washington Post*, April 22, 2015. www.washingtonpost.com/local/education/pa-schools-are-the-nations-most-inequitable-the-new-governor-wants-to-fix-that/2015/04/22/3d2f4e3e-e441-11e4-81ea-0649268f729e_story.html.
2. "Pennsylvania Supreme Court Strikes down State's Congressional Districts." *CBS News*, January 23, 2018. www.cbsnews.com/news/pennsylvania-supreme-court-strikes-down-states-congressional-districts-gerrymandering/.
3. Elizabeth Behrman. "Landmark Lawsuit Challenges How Pennsylvania Funds Its Public Schools | Pittsburgh Post-Gazette." *Pittsburgh Post-Gazette*, September 3, 2019. www.post-gazette.com/business/bop/2019/09/03/Debate-continues-over-public-school-funding-in-Pennsylvania/stories/201908050109.
4. "Poorest Big US City Endorses Predictable Work Schedules." *US News & World Report*, December 6, 2018. www.usnews.com/news/best-states/pennsylvania/articles/2018-12-06/poorest-big-us-city-endorses-predictable-work-schedules.
5. Robert D. Lane, Jr., Laura Bottaro Galier, and Kevin Greenberg. "Philadelphia Legal Representation in Landlord Tenant Court Ordinance Passes." *The National Law Review*, November 19, 2019. www.natlawreview.com/article/philadelphia-enacts-right-to-counsel-evictions-law.
6. Samantha Melamed. "Philly's House of Correction, a 'Dungeon,' to Close by 2020." *The Philadelphia Inquirer*, April 18, 2018. www.inquirer.com/philly/news/pennsylvania/philadelphia/house-of-correction-closing-department-of-prisons-20180418.html.

The Path to a Political Majority   123

7. "Philadelphia Is Ending a Major Contract with ICE." *All Things Considered*. National Public Radio, July 28, 2018. www.npr.org/2018/07/28/633460392/philadelphia-is-ending-a-major-contract-with-ice.
8. Julia Terruso. "The Blue Wave Crashed Down on Pennsylvania Again, as Voters from Philly to Delaware County Turned Left." *The Philadelphia Inquirer*, November 6, 2019. www.inquirer.com/news/pennsylvania-2019-election-results-20191106.html.
9. Greg Windle. "What Does Helen Gym's Resounding Vote Total Mean for Council and Education?" *The Notebook*, May 29, 2019. https://thenotebook.org/articles/2019/05/29/what-does-helen-gyms-resounding-vote-total-mean-for-council-and-education/.
10. Sean Collins Walsh, and Laura McCrystal. "Kendra Brooks Captures a Philadelphia City Council Seat in a Historic Win for the Working Families Party and Philly Progressives." *The Philadelphia Inquirer*, November 6, 2019. www.inquirer.com/politics/election/philly-city-council-at-large-kendra-brooks-working-families-party-republicans-20191106.html.

25 Guaranteed Quality, Comprehensive Health Care Coverage From Cradle to Grave

Stephanie Nakajima

I grew up in the United States, where it's not uncommon to hear people say they feel "lucky" to have health insurance. I think that's why it took me some time to realize that I had a right to health care, and that this right had been violated by my country.

After years of being uninsured or very poorly insured, I moved to Japan, where I was included in the public health insurance scheme practically upon landing. Finally, I was able to get my asthma under control, have a regular supply of my meds, and unload the constant dread of receiving a huge medical bill should I get hurt or have an asthma attack. The relief was overwhelming. A year later, when I considered moving back to the United States, I had grown accustomed to having reliable insurance and decided that if I was going to throw myself back into the mercy of the American health care system, it would only be on the terms that I was there to fuck it up.

I'm the Director of Communications at Healthcare-NOW, which organizes grassroots campaigns for single-payer health care, or Medicare for All. We work with chapters in over 20 states across the country that work to pass single payer on the national and, in some areas, the state level. We envision a system in which everyone—regardless of documentation status, employment, gender, age, or disability—is guaranteed quality, comprehensive health care coverage from cradle to grave.

One of the advantages, if you can call it that, of our movement is that almost everyone is affected by the health care system. That's why it consistently ranks among the top concerns of voters; rising health care costs are burdening not just lower income families but increasingly middle- and even upper-middle-income people, and just being insured offers less and less protection from these costs. This makes talking about health care different, and in some ways easier, than talking to voters about other issues like climate change, which can feel more abstract. So rather than memorizing a list of talking points, it's better to start with your own experience, and get people to talk about theirs as well.

We at Healthcare-NOW have a "How to Tell Your Story" training that we go through with all of our organizers. This doesn't stem from an ideological stance about building power or the importance of making connections; we use storytelling because it's proven to work. You're going to want to approach voters with *your own reasons* about why you are in this movement, why you're knocking on their door right now. Having a 30-second story that communicates your values through your concrete lived experience will help get a two-way conversation going. It's so much more compelling to talk about your experiences rather than to generally moralize about "health care as a human right." It's the ultimate in "show, don't tell," and people will respond by opening up about their own experiences.

Some of you will know right away the moment you decided to become an activist; others may have to take more time reflecting on your experiences to better understand the path you took. The years I spent surviving were not spent examining the ways in which our systems were curtailing my rights. In crafting that story, it might be helpful to reflect on your current and past experiences with health care access. Have your premiums or deductibles gone up, and how has that affected your budget or ability to pay for treatment? Have you ever spent time talking on the phone with an insurance company to get a treatment authorized, a mistake resolved, or a bill negotiated? Have you ever been in a job just for the health care benefits it provided for you or your family, or worked an extra job just to pay for health care costs? Has anyone in your close network of friends or family experienced any of these things?

Once grievances have been shared and affirmed, it's easy to segue into the solution—Medicare for All. But here's what you don't want to do: launch into a policy presentation that includes the words "GDP" or "federal spending." A study commissioned by a coalition of progressive groups found that the three strongest arguments for single payer are that people would no longer die because they couldn't afford medicine or care; that the United States would no longer be the only developed country without a universal health system; and that families would no longer struggle to provide long-term care for seniors and people with disabilities. By March 2020, the COVID-19 pandemic underscored these arguments and increased the awareness that all our health futures are intertwined.

Note that arguments about overall health care system costs, how doctors or hospitals would be paid, or administrative waste are all missing from the list. Advocates of universal health care are often drawn to these bigger-picture benefits of a Medicare for All system, rather than raising consciousness that people's basic dignity is violated by our current health care system. Fortunately, the most resonant arguments for single payer are also ones that distinguish it from alternative health reforms, such as the public option, that centrist candidates are using to temper our momentum. Talking about the stakes—people's lives and livelihoods—helps to make the case for a guarantee rather than an "option."

Of course, if the voters you talk to bring up concerns about the cost of the health care system on the federal scale, then that'd be a great time to talk about the cost savings of a single-payer health care plan. But lead with what they care about—ask for and listen to their experiences.

Voters are likely to have heard talking points from the opposition and may need reassurance or help with fact-checking. Fear-mongering about tax hikes or eliminating private insurance used to be a strategy exclusive to Republicans, but as Medicare for All gains support, we're finding that such lines of attack are increasingly being used by Democratic politicians as well. As of this writing, here are some of the most common opposition lines and the ways we'd suggest tackling them:

Will Medicare for All–Style Programs Raise Taxes on the Middle Class?

Medicare for All establishes health care as a publicly funded right. Your current premiums, deductibles, and co-pays—which increase every year by an unpredictable percentage—would be replaced by low, stable taxes. Are you in the bottom 80% of earners? Then this means savings, because lower and middle-income people pay more as a percentage of their income for health care than do the wealthy.

We're going to have to confront our tax paranoia if we're going to equitably finance health care (or anything else for that matter), so if you're asked about higher taxes, own it! Public financing is a benefit of Medicare for All—not a drawback—because it's *the fairest way* of financing our health care. Asking everyone to pay *proportional to their means* would be a huge improvement upon the current system, which cruelly asks those who are sicker, female, older, and low-income to pay disproportionately more.

I Have Good Health Benefits Through My Work. Why Would I Want Single-Payer Reform?

Many with excellent workplace health insurance have found that a serious illness or injury may cause them to lose their job, and subsequently their health insurance. This is a great time to talk or ask about personal experiences; here, I would talk about the stress my family endured after my dad lost his job—and the entire family's health insurance benefits—when he was 55, a difficult age to be quickly re-employed.

Employer health insurance has its drawbacks as well. Health insurance is simply another lever of control that employers have over you as an employee, and increasingly those benefits are less and less generous.

I'm a Senior—How Does Medicare for All Impact Those of Us With Medicare?

Medicare for All would dramatically improve Medicare for you! It would *expand the program* to include comprehensive long-term care coverage, including at-home services and supports, as well as nursing-home care; this would be life-changing for you and tens of millions of other seniors and their families, who would no longer be made destitute by the care they need.

The Congressional Medicare for All Act adds hearing, dental, and vision coverage, and eliminates premiums, co-pays, and deductibles. This means huge savings; currently, seniors are spending about 41% of the average Social Security benefit on health care. That'd be a game changer for people on a fixed income!

Won't Medicare for All Lead to Long Wait Times and Rationing of Care?

No. Every health care system, whether public or private, has to ration its resources, but in the United States we ration based on ability to pay—leaving millions outside of the system—while single-payer systems ration based on medical need.

We think of wait times and rationing as something that happens in other countries, but ironically we actually have longer wait times for primary care, mental health, and even emergency care. Ask the voter, "Have you had to wait a long time for a doctor's visit, or skipped it altogether because of cost?" And provide the answer, "Your insurer has a fee schedule of co-pays or deductibles set up as a barrier to care, and restricts the providers you can see through what's called a 'network'—giving you a narrower choice of doctors, and therefore less opportunities to book a time. *That's* rationing! It happens right here in the United States. We can end networks and out of pocket costs with Medicare for All."

Political Feasibility Concerns

Generally, voters agree with Medicare for All in principle, but feel like the issue is too polarizing to be passable. Here's how we usually tackle these questions:

I've Heard That Most People Really Want to Keep Their Private Health Insurance.

A majority of respondents (55%) support "eliminating private health insurance" when told they can keep their choice of doctors and hospitals.

Negative feelings are actually much higher around private insurance; 70% of people are opposed to allowing employers to change or eliminate an employee's health insurance against the employee's wishes. Yet this is how private health insurance works! Medicare for All would take health coverage out of the hands of employers—exactly as survey respondents prefer.

A Public Option Would Be a Great Stepping Stone.

A public option would do little to address the problem with our health care system, and wouldn't set up any infrastructure useful in transitioning to Medicare for All. Studies have shown that public option proposals would barely make a dent in the rate of the uninsured, wouldn't help anyone with skimpy private insurance, and would do very little to bring down costs.

A Public Option Gives People the Choice to Transition.

Right now, employers and conservative state governments determine our health care coverage for us. A public option would preserve this, and simply provide an additional choice for these employers to make on behalf of the working class and poor people, including plans with high-deductibles and co-payments. Under Medicare for All, employers and state governments would lose the ability to make insurance choices for us, as comprehensive coverage would be provided as a right for all residents regardless of their employment situation or the state we live in.

Get Involved

Healthcare-NOW doesn't endorse any candidates or do Get Out the Vote work; because the industry is so deeply invested in both of our major political parties, we're going to need a mass movement that includes people from all over the political spectrum to hold their legislators accountable for passing Medicare for All. You can get involved in that movement by joining Healthcare-NOW.

Prepare further for your canvassing conversations here, or take an online organizing training: www.singlepayerschool.healthcare-now.org/

Part IV
Turnout!

26 How to Turn a Person Into a Voter[1]

LaTosha Brown and Cliff Albright

All year, our group, Black Voters Matter Fund,[2] crisscrosses the South and a couple of states in the North, often focusing on progressive pockets in red states to find people who have been ignored.

We've learned how to turn community members into committed voters. In 2016, the country saw the lowest presidential turnout rate for Blacks since 2000, but in 2017, Black voters in Alabama shocked the country by defeating Roy Moore. Since that time, in our work we've seen enormous success in local and statewide races, such as those which elected Alabama's first Black mayor in Montgomery, Alabama, and which helped Alabama's first Black mayor, and which helped Louisiana Governor John Bel Edwards win re-election.

And although our approach is rooted in black people in the South, our model is one that any party or politician or group looking to increase turnout—or to mobilize the 7 in 10 eligible voters who have stayed at home during the primaries—should use.

Let Folks Know That They Are Loved and That They Matter

We don't come to our community members like they are just votes to be rounded up or counted like jelly beans. We're coming in as friends, with hugs and love. Through love, we are able to emphasize that this is a collective process based on our interconnections and mutual hopes. In an election cycle marked by the trauma of the coronavirus and a tendency to socially distance ourselves, it will be important to remember that physical distance need not mean psychological distance.

Our web of mutuality can never give way to an individualism that denies love, and our search for victories defined narrowly should never force us to take organizing shortcuts that fail to communicate that each person we contact matters.

Remind People They Have Political Power

Some marginalized communities view power as a dirty word, something not to be desired because it has been used to perpetuate racism and other injustices. We always tell people, "Power at its best is love implementing the demands of justice," as the Rev. Dr. Martin Luther King, Jr., said.

If politics is defined as the process of distributing power, then voting is a critical way a community shapes how that power is distributed. Voting lets us choose elected officials who, in turn, make choices that affect our lives.

You turn a person into a voter by helping her see this. By asking her what she cares about and what she needs from her government. In that way, you connect her to her political power. And you show her that, to exercise that power, she has got to vote.

Don't Parachute In

Even if a place is tiny and rural and practically off the map, we always assume there's already a culture of activism to tap into. To start, we sit in a circle with local leaders and ask questions: What do people want? What are the community's strengths? What is the civil rights history here? What are the local conflicts?

Our local partners, most of whom are black women, are essential because they know their community's needs best. We support their phone banking, peer-to-peer texting, canvassing, and voter education efforts. When we leave, we ask: Are more people engaged than before the election? Have we strengthened local leaders to do what they do best?

In many of these areas, there are still remnants of the civil rights movement. This can be a good thing, as when legends from the Student Nonviolent Coordinating Committee pass down their advice. But there can also be trauma from lynchings and other brutality that's passed down from generation to generation and shrouded in silence. This can make our work trickier, but the key is to really get to know a place.

Center Local Issues

Ask people what they care about and what their community needs from their government. One summer, we chatted with a nursing assistant at a restaurant in Americus, Georgia, who had just decided to sit out the midterms. We asked her a few questions and learned that some of her family members didn't have good access to health care. One even had to drive some 100 miles to get to the nearest hospital; eight rural hospitals have closed in Georgia since 2008,[3] more than in any other state except Texas and Tennessee.

We asked her, "Do you know what's happening with Medicaid?" She didn't. So we explained that if Georgia followed the more than 30 states that have expanded Medicaid, rural hospitals could stay open, and it could create thousands of new health care jobs. Her face lit up. She walked across the street to our bus and filled out a voter registration form. And she persuaded her friend to do the same.

Let Folks Know They Matter 365 Days a Year

You can't just show up in September or October. You have to get your hands dirty throughout the year. If you haven't, make sure you're working closely with someone who has. It's not sexy work, and the rest of the country isn't paying attention. But you can't ignore communities for 11 months and then spend 30 days trying to convince them to flip a state and save the world.

Being engaged 365 days a year also means that you don't pack your bags after the race is over. And it also means supporting down-ballot races that impact people on a daily basis.

Don't Play the Shame Game

Many voters, especially black voters, who sit out elections are not apathetic. Indeed, they are passionate about why they're not voting, and even more so about what they want from their government. It is precisely because their hopes have been unfulfilled—left to dry up like a raisin in the sun—that they choose to stay home.

We're not coming in to wag our fingers. We never try to convince people they're wrong or shame them. That doesn't work. We listen and validate their feelings. We even admit that sometimes we don't feel like voting. This is part of our strategy: You can make a more durable connection with someone if you empathize.

Know the Culture

We firmly believe that culture trumps strategy. Many "experts" have implemented comprehensive strategic plans that fail to achieve results because they didn't build upon—or even worse, were inconsistent with—community culture. We always communicate in a way that our audience can relate to. Often that communication isn't about words, but about intangibles such as the role of faith, or the importance of food gatherings as a unifying tradition.

We start our meetings with songs that people who grew up in the black church or around the freedom movement know, like "Keep Your Eyes on the Prize." And if we're at a football tailgate party and our crowd's a little younger, we count on Kendrick Lamar to assure us that "we gon' be all right." We play these songs because they fill our spirits and affirm who we are, not because they're entertainment. Historically, even when we've had nothing else, we've always had our culture, and often that was enough.

Notes

1. This is a revised and updated version of the essay "How to Turn a Person Into a Voter" by LaTosha Brown and Cliff Albright that originally appeared in *The New York Times* on October 27, 2018.
2. Blackvotersmatter. "Black Voters Matter Fund." Accessed March 19, 2020. www.blackvotersmatterfund.org.
3. Abby Goodnough. "Stacey Abrams Hopes Medicaid Expansion Can Be a Winning Issue in Rural Georgia—The New York Times." *The New York Times*, October 20, 2018. www.nytimes.com/2018/10/20/health/medicaid-georgia-abrams-midterms.html.

27 Eyes South! The Ins and Outs of Voting From Abroad

Deborah Klebansky and Kira Moodliar

Of the three million U.S. citizens of voting age living abroad in 2016, only about 208,000 voted in the last presidential election, a humble turnout of 7%.[1] Think about the 2016 popular vote: with Trump losing by nearly three million votes but winning the Electoral College with a razor-thin margin of about 80,000 votes in three battleground states, overseas voting may make a huge difference.[2]

We are American students who have been living in Montreal for the entirety of the Trump administration. More than 600,000 U.S. citizens of voting age live in Canada.[3] Our university alone has 2,267 Americans attending, making them *our* specific constituents. With nearly a million Americans of all ages living in Canada—more than the number of Americans living in the seven smallest American states—turnout work here can be pivotal.

Many obstacles explain the low turnout rate. These include the overcomplicated balloting process. In fact, only 88% of citizens who requested absentee ballots in 2016 actually received them.[4] Further, the absence of a federalized election process hurts absentee balloting, leaving would-be voters mired in arcane, state-specific rules and deadlines. Even with these facts, voters abroad could have a serious impact.

For the past three years, we struggled to find our place in domestic politics while abroad, all while under the daily barrage of news concerning the state of affairs at home. Nonetheless, our activism, particularly in environmental justice work in Montreal, together with U.S. political organizations abroad, have demonstrated to us how much we can do in the elections, even at a distance. Our social-movement activism and our community-building work leaves us confident that we can increase voter turnout abroad.

As volunteers, we can reach American citizens currently in the United States through phone banking and letter writing. However, organizing Americans living in Canada is less straightforward. It is difficult to canvass American voters dispersed across the city in which we live, so our voter registration work is confined to registering fellow students to vote. The general difficulties of absentee voting aggravate the challenge of increasing turnout. To counteract these difficulties, we will address two topics: (1) the rules for registering to vote and for casting absentee ballots; and (2) community-building among U.S. citizens living north of the border. With our eyes focused squarely on how we can make a difference at the polls, we need to turn out more overseas voters and ensure that their vote counts in 2020.

Nuts and Bolts: How to Vote Abroad

Let's start with the boring but necessary facts.[5] Voting abroad is not as simple as finding time to vote on election day. Since many students are unregistered when they leave home, registering to vote is the first step toward voting abroad. This step can be complicated, but it is very doable.

Each state has its own deadlines. States also have varying regulations for receiving, submitting, and processing voter registration and absentee ballot applications, and for the processing ballots themselves. Voting in the general election *is* through one's home state.

1. **Make sure you are registered** (and know the registration deadlines for you to be eligible to vote in a specific election):
   To check your registration status, use www.Vote.org. You have to submit (1) your registered name, (2) your last recalled registered address, and (3) an email address. This site validates your name on a voter register, *but not your address*. This allows you to confirm your registration and that you have not been purged from the voter registry. You can also see if you need to update your legal address.
   To register, or change your address in the United States, we recommend using www.VotingFromAbroad.org.
2. **Apply for an absentee ballot**:
   We recommend three sites for this process: www.VoteFromAbroad.org, www.Vote.org, and your county elections website. Check the National Association of Counties website to find your county by entering your city or zip code.[6]

Eyes South! 139

3. **Receive and submit your ballot:**
 Depending on the state, your ballot may be mailed, emailed, or generated via online link. Despite the 21st-century means of receiving the ballot, in nearly all cases you must send a *paper ballot by mail* with a post-mark of a certain time before any election day. Depending on the voter ID laws of your state, you may have to include a photocopy of your ID with your ballot.[7] Luckily, all absentee ballots for federal elections are already postage paid.[8]
4. **If you do not receive your ballot:**
 If you do not receive your ballot (after applying before the deadline) three days preceding election day, you must use a Federal Write-in Absentee Ballot (FWAB). For more information about FWABs, please go to Vote.org.

Building Community Abroad to Maximize Turnout

On November 4, 2016, McGill University students held an election-watch party, anticipating a victorious night. Instead, the atmosphere of the packed bar grew quieter and quieter as the night wore on, for obvious reasons. The atmosphere might have been morose, but Americans abroad were huddling together, offering hugs and condolences. The energy of the room shifted to one of support and empathy.

More importantly, after that night, the community of Americans abroad—like many compatriots as home—moved from being passive viewers to being impassioned citizens. In the middle of Montreal, there was this odd patriotism, not for the new president, but from a sense of collective fate—our realities were going to change. We had to work harder to combat our new political reality. Unlike many vulnerable communities on American soil, we might not be living our day-to-day lives in fear, but we now had to leverage our distance, our "privilege," if you will, and discover the potential to organize and support changemaking.

Moreover, as U.S. citizens living in Canada, we have a unique vantage point: we know the realities of Canadian social and political life. In the debates that happen in the United States over Canada, we can be the truth tellers. For example, we know first-hand the strengths and weaknesses of the Canadian health system. Even with conservative swings in Ontario and Quebec, Canadians are not looking for cut backs or privatization; they are seeking improvements to the public sector. In matters of the environment in Canada, much of the oil and fossil-fuel infrastructure being promoted here are largely funded by

U.S. interests. A continuation of the Trump agenda will only intensify such undemocratic projects—a further insult to land defenders and First Nations across Canada. This upcoming election will have international consequences regarding climate justice, foreign policy, and social services. American voters abroad have the chance to promote positive outcomes rather than passively await condemnation.

The community that emerged as we felt aggrieved after 2016's ballot must now be mobilized to register voters, network with those voters, and ensure that everyone "shows up" in November.

Notes

1. FORS MARSH Group. "2016 Overseas Citizen Population Analysis Report." *Federal Voting Assistance Program*, September 2018. www.fvap.gov/info/reports-surveys/overseas-citizen-population-analysis.
2. Philip Bump. "Donald Trump Will Be President Thanks to 80,000 People in Three States." *The Washington Post*, December 1, 2016. www.washingtonpost.com/news/the-fix/wp/2016/12/01/donald-trump-will-be-president-thanks-to-80000-people-in-three-states/.
3. FORS MARSH Group. "2016 Overseas Citizen Population Analysis Report." *Federal Voting Assistance Program*, September 2018. www.fvap.gov/info/reports-surveys/overseas-citizen-population-analysis.
4. FORS MARSH Group. "2016 Overseas Citizen Population Analysis Report." *Federal Voting Assistance Program*, September 2018, p. 20. www.fvap.gov/uploads/FVAP/Reports/FVAP-2016-OCPA-FINAL-Report.pdf.
5. See the *Turnout!* website for a short essay describing myths about voting from abroad: http://emergencyelection.org.
6. National Association of Countries. "County Explorer." n.d. https://ce.naco.org/.
7. Vote.org. "Voter ID Laws." n.d. www.vote.org/voter-id-laws/.
8. Federal Voting Assistance Program. "Absentee Voting Overview." Accessed March 5, 2020. www.fvap.gov/citizen-voter/overview.

28 Voter Assemblies to Protect the Vote

Ben Manski and Suren Moodliar

> *I REMEMBER the systemic election fraud and voting rights violations in recent presidential contests, and I am willing to take action this year to protect free and fair elections.*
>
> *I SUPPORT efforts to protect the right to vote leading up to and on Election Day, November 3, 2020.*
>
> *If necessary, I PLEDGE to join nationwide pro-democracy protests starting on the next day, either in my community, in key states where fraud occurred, or in Washington, D.C., and if necessary, to demand a recount, investigation, and criminal prosecutions of those responsible.*
> —No More Stolen Elections! Pledge of Action for 2020

On November 22, 2000, as ballots were being recounted in Miami-Dade and Broward counties in Florida, Republican Party operatives forcibly entered the elections offices, halting the ongoing manual recount. The political stakes could not have been higher. This was a presidential election, the outcome of which turned on Florida's electoral votes. Whatever the strategic mistakes of the Democratic Party contender, Al Gore, it was the actions of the Republican operatives that were decisive. Labeled "a bourgeois riot" by the *Wall Street Journal*, off-duty GOP staffers forced the election out of voter's hands and into a stacked Supreme Court.[1] In turn, the Court selected the climate change denier and Iraq War architect George W. Bush, a candidate who had actually lost the popular vote both in Florida and across the country. With their choice, the five Supreme Court justices postponed action on catastrophic climate change by at least two decades, at the very moment such action would have counted the most and cost the least; they also burdened current and future generations with war casualties and debt.

For most of us, voting is at once an institutional and individual activity. We enter the voting booth alone. The Florida recounts of 2000 and 2018,[2] the Wisconsin recounts of 2011 and 2012,[3] the Green Party-initiated presidential recounts of 2004 and 2016,[4] the 2018 North Carolina election fraud Dowless case,[5] the egregious voter-roll purges that impacted Georgia's 2018 gubernatorial election,[6] and many other cases all indicate that voting is never just an individual action, nor is it an adequately protected institution. In many cases, Hanlon's razor—*never attribute to malice that which stupidity can explain*—applies. However, the purging of voter rolls, gerrymandering, and other forms of vote suppression (including election day voter intimidation) all provide evidence of deeper structural problems. Not for nothing does Richard L. Hasen, a leading scholar of law and democracy, note that "the United States is almost alone among mature democracies in allowing the foxes to guard the henhouse."[7]

Building on the work of the Liberty Foundation for the Democratic Revolution, its allies, and its networks,[8] we provide a how-to guide to the creation of voter assemblies to protect and expand voter sovereignty. The experience of committed activists is that hard-won voting rights can and must be protected. Directly. By voters. Themselves.

Being prepared matters: In 2016, the presidential election came down to a few communities in Wisconsin, Michigan, and Pennsylvania. Preparing voter assemblies in these communities—places like Detroit, Milwaukee, and Philadelphia—made possible an immediate organized response and contributed to the strength of the grassroots recount efforts eventually led by the Stein campaign.

Of course, Donald Trump has never publicly admitted that he lost the popular vote in 2016. And he warned of violence by his supporters in the event that he was declared the loser of the Electoral College. Looking ahead to November of 2020, many observers are concerned about the likelihood that violence and intimidation will be deployed to thwart the will of the voters.[9] Even with this Trump-induced uncertainty, other threats remain, including both the knowable and the unpredictable consequences of the global pandemic and other "natural disasters."[10]

What Are Voter Assemblies?[11]

Voter assemblies are *self-organized* community spaces where people come together to discuss reports of fraud and voter suppression that threaten election integrity, and to take action when necessary to stop elections from being stolen. Although these assemblies may be

Voter Assemblies to Protect the Vote 143

created at any point in time, it is best to plan ahead and to schedule your first assembly for the day after the election. This year, our federal elections take place on November 3. The best day for you to organize your first voter assembly is therefore Wednesday, November 4.[12]

This election is being threatened by unverifiable voting machines, voter ID laws that disenfranchise millions of eligible voters, and restrictive election laws for third-party candidates and voters who wish to vote early, as well as many other forms of voter suppression that we are likely to witness on and before November 3. It is entirely possible that states may change voting rules and procedures in response to real or perceived public health or other emergencies. Your voter assembly may also have to be organized online, using social media channels and other communications systems. Voter assemblies allow us to sidestep the mainstream media's relative neglect of election integrity issues and to connect with lawyers, election experts, and others in our communities who share the same concerns about fair and just elections. By bringing us together to meet face-to-face, voter assemblies empower us to speak and act collectively against election fraud.

What we describe here is not just "a good idea." We are describing what voter assemblies have already accomplished.

In July of 2004, a coalition of democracy, civil rights, and peace groups, led by Liberty Tree, Code Pink, Global Exchange, and United for Peace & Justice, circulated a No Stolen Elections! Pledge of Action signed by 70 leading voices from across the progressive movement.[13] In the following months, 23,735 people signed the pledge, and many of those pledge signers participated in preparing assemblies and other actions in 82 communities across the country.

Over election night and into the morning of November 3, 2004, a team of election integrity experts met hourly to assess reports of election irregularities and voter suppression. A little after midnight, that team issued a report determining that the level of election manipulation documented in Ohio, Florida, and Wisconsin had risen to a level of fraud that could possibly determine the outcome of the presidential election. Later that morning, the team released a follow-up report indicating that election fraud in Ohio was likely. Based on these assessments, the coalition called for voter assemblies to protest and to mobilize support for a potential recount in Ohio.

Over the following weeks and months, the volunteers mobilized through No Stolen Elections! joined with others in supporting the recount initiated by Liberty Tree Fellow and 2004 Green presidential nominee David Cobb. Together, they organized protests across the country, raised money, and traveled to Ohio to lend their labor. The short-term impacts of those mobilizations included the convictions of several election administration officials, the end of Ohio Secretary of State Ken Blackwell's political career, and the Conyers Report on the 2004 presidential election, which concluded that voter repression and voting machine manipulation had been deliberate and systematic.[14] To millions of Americans, it became clear that while Bush may have won the popular vote, he only won the Electoral College through fraud. Longer-term outcomes included the formation of scores of new local, regional, and national election integrity and voting rights organizations, as well as heightened awareness of problems posed by electronic voting systems—particularly those owned and operated by private corporations like Diebold.[15] In some states, these grassroots groups have won important victories that increased voting access, made hand counting of ballots possible, and replaced plurality elections with ranked-choice voting.

The main takeaway from 2004 is this: Because tens of thousands of people were organized and prepared *in advance* to act *after election day* to protect the vote, fraud was confronted and public officials were held accountable; the struggle for democratic elections advanced. The lessons learned in 2004–2005 were taken and implemented again in later elections with the No More Stolen Elections! campaigns of the federal elections of 2008, 2012, and 2016, as well as the 2012 Wisconsin gubernatorial recall election and hand audit recount investigation. Each of those efforts prepared coordinated action by voters to safeguard voting rights and to contest election fraud. Because the threat posed to election integrity in 2020 is much more obvious and serious than any seen in recent memory, voters must scale up their preparations to defend the vote.

Given these stakes, we move next from the "what" to the "how"— a modest set of actions, readily accomplished, with the potential for national impact. In coordination with NoMoreStolenElections.org, the voter assemblies provide a space for authentic local concerns about voting irregularities and the election process to be clearly formulated and given a national platform. Your assemblies are *directly* accountable to you. The agenda evolves out of your concerns and "the big picture" of the 2020 election emerges out of a dialogue among assemblies.

Where Do I Start?

Several steps can take place in tandem. In general, you identify your networks and figure out how to tap into established ones. But you don't need anyone's permission! Get started, develop flexible plans, and be open to changing them based on what you consider good-faith feedback.

Choose a Good Location and Time

In November, you may prefer to use an indoor space. An accessible, public space such as a community center, publicly accessible government building, library, labor hall, or student union would be ideal. In warmer climates, accessible public spaces outside (parks, prominent plazas, or in front of civic buildings) may also be a good bet.

Next, choose a time on Wednesday, November 4 (*the day after the election*) to start your event. Depending on where you live you may want to have meet at around noon, or you may wish to schedule your meeting for when most people will be done with work, around 5:30 or 6 p.m.

Register the voter assembly at www.NoMoreStolenElections.org and include a link to any Facebook or other social media events you create for your voter assembly.

If circumstances prevent or limit in-person gatherings, organize an alternative or supplemental virtual gathering through some combination of conference calls, webinars, and other communications platforms (e.g., Zoom, Skype, MayFirst.coop, etc.). Each technology choice will have its idiosyncrasies and costs, even when nominally free. Each has a learning curve. Choices may exclude interested people. As such, advance preparation, deliberation, and transparent sharing of information about these online gatherings is critical. NoMoreStolenElections.org provides a guide to these services.

Should the elections move to mail-in balloting and/or other online formats, the voter assemblies will still need to be convened to document experiences and to respond to reports about those processes.

Social Media

Create a Facebook event for your voter assembly right away and ask all of your friends to invite their Facebook friends to the event. Name it something like "[Springfield] Voter Assembly." Then tweet about the event and include the link to the Facebook event in the tweet. It will be important to have as many people in-person at your voter assembly as possible. But setting up a Facebook event will allow you to include those who can't make it and also to stay in touch in case there are limits on travel (e.g., pandemic-related restrictions).

Also use other creative ways to publicize the assembly and its location. For instance, visit the venue beforehand and share a photo or video of it via a Facebook story, Instagram, Twitter, and other channels.

Build Your Networks and Community

Here are some suggestions for organizations to reach out to in advance. Find out about their voting rights and election integrity efforts. Invite them to participate in a post-election voter assembly:

- NAACP local chapters (www.naacp.org/find-local-unit/)
- League of Women Voters state branches (www.lwv.org/about-us/membership-local-leagues)
- Central labor councils and state federations of labor (https://aflcio.org/about-us/our-unions-and-allies/state-federations-and-central-labor-councils)
- College student associations (https://en.wikipedia.org/wiki/Category:Student_governments_in_the_United_States)
- Center for Popular Democracy partners (https://populardemocracy.org/our-partners) and People's Action members (https://peoplesaction.org/member-organizations/)
- Move to Amend local chapters (https://movetoamend.org/)
- Women's International League for Peace and Freedom state/local branches (https://wilpfus.org/contact/branch-directory)
- American Civil Liberties Union state branches (www.aclu.org/about/affiliates), National Lawyers Guild affiliates (www.nlg.org/chapters/), and chapters of the American Constitution Society (www.acslaw.org/acs-chapters/)
- Any nonpartisan Get Out the Vote efforts
- Other state and local election integrity organizations
- Peace and justice centers and networks

Through this outreach, you will learn about existing efforts by lawyers and various organizations to track voting and overcome election irregularities and voter suppression. Begin developing your own sense of how these problems are emerging in your region and state. Document credible reports. This will be important down the road.

Next: Build It

If all you are able to do is to schedule a voter assembly and do a little to spread the word, then do that. Some preparation is better than none at all. But you and your community will benefit if you are able to hold some organizing meetings in advance. Bring others into the process. Get more people involved in planning and publicizing your assembly. You won't regret it.

Organizing Meeting(s)

If possible, hold two organizing meetings in advance of election day. Your first meeting should probably be by invitation only. Who are the essential individuals and organizations that can help plan the agenda, publicity, and location of your voter assembly? Whose knowledge, experience, and network ties should be in the room?

Having had that first planning meeting, you might schedule a second meeting: A public forum ahead of election day to sensitize your community about the need to defend and demand democratic elections.

Again, this is up to you. Do what you can. Some preparation is better than none.

Flyers and Posters

Create a quick poster and/or quarter-sheet flyers with the information about the assembly. Put up the posters in public spaces such as coffee shops, community billboards, and street kiosks. Get a team of friends together on election day and distribute the flyers in high traffic areas (remember to stay at least 100 feet away from polling places so you don't make the poll workers nervous) or at public election result watching parties.

- Hand-drawing or even creating collages that can be copied are often very effective for reaching friends and neighbors.
- Easy online sites are available for posters; free, easy-to-use poster and flyer apps for your phones and tablets can be found in Android and iOS stores.
- Ideally, your poster can be dual-purposed into a banner for social media.

Social Media and Other Spread-the-Word Methods

- **Traditional social media** that your friends and community normally use are ideal and quick ways to get out the word since virtually no learning curve is involved. However, do be sure to supplement these with other methods since social media can

easily exclude whole sectors of people who may otherwise be very interested in protecting the vote.
- **Blogs** are also a good way to spread the word about your voter assembly. If you don't have a blog, then ask around to find out if anyone you know would be willing to write a blog post about the importance of acting now to protect the integrity of this election.
- **Emails** remain among the best ways to spread the word about the voter assembly. Ask local grassroots organizations to send out an email announcement to their listservs.
- **Community and public radio and cable shows** may have call-in segments or accessible producers; take advantage of those opportunities.
- **Community, faith, labor, or club newsletters** may have sympathetic editors; reach out and see what advance publicity you can get.
- **Community calendars** in local newspapers and blogs usually will accept postings 7–15 days in advance. Don't miss their deadlines.

Running the Voter Assembly

On election night, the No More Stolen Elections! team will work with other election-integrity and voting-rights experts to assess the many reports coming in from across the country and to produce a series of short reports. You will be able to use these reports as a basis for discussion and action at your voter assembly. The website will also include a sample agenda for how to structure the assembly, one based on the objective to share national information with local participants and to bring local and state-wide concerns forward for sharing with the broader community. Remember to collect everyone's contact information and set a date for the next gathering

After the Assembly

Let the world know how things went! Pass along any photos/contact information you gathered at the assembly to us and your other national networks.

- Report back using the same channels you used to advertise your assembly.
- Let all the organizations that you contacted know what was decided.

Above all else, regardless of the outcomes, keep your community together. Keep organizing. Keep meeting as needed. Keep the communication lines open with election attorneys and voting-rights organizations.[16] And keep on moving forward with an agenda for democratizing our system of governance.[17]

On Whom We Must Rely

We have learned some important lessons about U.S. elections since 2000.

We know now, even if we should have known it before, that some in power will flagrantly subvert the will of the electorate to retain their power. This is particularly true among the increasing number of public figures who advocate for minority rule and are openly hostile to the very idea of democracy.

We have learned that in times of crisis, some politicians choose to protect the continuity of the political order *against the voting rights of their own supporters*. Vice President Gore justified his decision to abandon the Florida recount as an act of virtue in defense of state stability. In 2004, Senator John Kerry likewise reneged on his promise to fight for his voters. And again, in 2016, despite warning that Trump posed a mortal threat to democracy and acknowledging widespread evidence of fraud, Senator Hillary Clinton backed away from her repeated pledge to fight "to count every vote."

We have seen that when voters act together to defend our voting rights and to demand democratic elections, we make ourselves heard. We force recounts. We expose election fraud. We bring public officials to account. We build power. We democratize election laws.

This year, the right to vote and to have our votes counted will come into contact with an incumbent who admires dictators and monarchs and who has openly allied with white supremacists. It would be madness to invest everything into turning out the vote and nothing into preparing for the days following the elections. To do that would be to deliberately forget all we have learned. It would mean ignoring what we know about the dangers of this moment. And it would be unnecessary because we have an alternative. We can organize voter assemblies in advance. We can rely on each other. And we must.

Notes

1. Michael E. Miller. "'It's Insanity!': How the 'Brooks Brothers Riot' Killed the 2000 Recount in Miami." *Washington Post*, November 15, 2018.

www.washingtonpost.com/history/2018/11/15/its-insanity-how-brooks-brothers-riot-killed-recount-miami/.
2. David Smiley. "How Florida's 2018 Recount Unfolded from Start to Finish | Miami Herald." *Miami Herald*, November 20, 2018. www.miamiherald.com/news/politics-government/state-politics/article221815280.html.
3. For a contemporary news reports, please see the archive hosted on Google Drive. https://drive.google.com/drive/folders/1mFXjUi8Wfd WzXkGF0g3y_X8yBXX5KMy5.
4. Steve Eder. "Stein Ends Recount Bid, but Says It Revealed Flaws in Voting System." *The New York Times*, December 13, 2016, sec. U.S. www.nytimes.com/2016/12/13/us/stein-ends-recount-bid-but-says-it-revealed-flaws-in-voting-system.html.
5. "North Carolina GOP Operative Faces New Felony Charges That Allege Ballot Fraud." *NPR.Org*, July 30, 2019. www.npr.org/2019/07/30/746800630/north-carolina-gop-operative-faces-new-felony-charges-that-allege-ballot-fraud.
6. Zak Cheney-Rice. "Georgia Is Really Good at Making It Hard for Black People to Vote, Study Finds." *Intelligencer*, December 13, 2019. https://nymag.com/intelligencer/2019/12/georgia-voter-suppression-under-kemp.html.
7. Richard L. Hasen. *The Voting Wars: From Florida 2000 to the Next Election Meltdown.* New Haven: Yale University Press, 2012.
8. The Liberty Tree Foundation describes itself as "committed to building a democracy movement for the U.S.A." and "to provide vital support to grassroots campaigns for democratic reform in many areas of American life, and bring those campaigns together to form a united movement for democracy." LibertyTreeFoundation.org.
9. Martin Longman, and Daniel Block. "How Trump Could Lose the Election and Remain President." *Washington Monthly*, April 7, 2019. https://washingtonmonthly.com/magazine/april-may-june-2019/how-trump-could-lose-the-election-and-remain-president/.
10. We place "natural disasters" in quotation marks because many of the worst consequences of these disasters are more attributable to social arrangements, public policy, and even malice or profiteering.
11. Much of the following text is drawn from materials and handbook created by us and our colleagues for the No More Stolen Elections! project of the Liberty Tree Foundation for the Democratic Revolution.
12. If procedures and facts on the ground change (e.g., through the increased use of mail-in balloting), it may be necessary to convene sooner in order to monitor the process and guard against procedures that may undermine the will of the would-be voters.
13. Initial Signatories. "No Stolen Elections! Pledge of Action." Accessed April 3, 2020. https://web.archive.org/web/20050204030508/http://nov3.us/initialsignatories.php.
14. See John Conyers and Anita Miller, eds. *What Went Wrong in Ohio: The Conyers Report on the 2004 Presidential Election.* Chicago: Academy Chicago Publishers, 2005; Fitrakis, Robert. "First Criminal Convictions from Ohio's Stolen 2004 Election Confirm Recount Was Rigged." *Columbus Free Press*, January 27, 2007. https://freepress.org/article/

Voter Assemblies to Protect the Vote 151

first-criminal-convictions-ohios-stolen-2004-election-confirm-recount-was-rigged.
15. Although Diebold has since exited the voting-machines market, strong concerns remain about the industry and the corporation that dominates it; see Jessica Huseman, "The Market for Voting Machines Is Broken. This Company Has Thrived in It." *ProPublica*, October 28, 2019. www.propublica.org/article/the-market-for-voting-machines-is-broken-this-company-has-thrived-in-it.
16. Earlier, in "Build your networks and community," we shared information about several networks and national organizations of lawyers. Most have local and/or state chapters. Be ready to communicate with them and document your findings including, where possible, as much specific information about perceived violations. Recording the date, time, and place of specific incidents together with the contact information of all parties and witnesses will be helpful starting points for the attorneys. Similarly, any additional documentation, including photos of forms and paperwork or recordings of incidents, should be preserved and backed up.
17. We must ask whether U.S. elections are free and fair based on democratic norms: are "we the people" actually governing ourselves? By this set of standards, the existing electoral framework in the United States is itself suspect and must be democratized. See the *Turnout!* website for a short essay on the "Voter Bill of Rights" process: http://emergencyelection.org.

29 A Letter to U.S. College Students

Conor L. Hicks, Conner Coles, Julianna Carbone, Morgan Jemtrud, Sophia Carter, Audrey Vas, Hannah LeBeau, Kara Johansen, and John Gehman

Introduction

Every once in a while, America arrives at a crossroads. The decisions made in these moments ripple across our society and send a message to the world. We're forced to ask ourselves: What do we want our country to stand for? Who do we want to be when we wake up in the morning? Neither question has a simple answer, but both are critical to the democratic experiment we cherish.

It's no secret that our democracy is in crisis. President Trump and congressional Republicans have waged an unrelenting assault on the very institutions they claim to support. The president seeks to demean, intimidate, and marginalize people of color, women, LGBTQ+ Americans, and countless others, while Republicans in Congress remain silent or actively cheer him on. While professing devotion to "hard-working Americans," Trump pursues policies that place their livelihoods in jeopardy. He sees cruelty and corruption as virtues and dismisses compassion as weakness. He seeks to undermine the rule of law and uses the powers of the presidency to punish his opponents. We know it's been an exhausting three years, with every scandal chipping away at our collective capacity for outrage. We're tired, we're angry, and we're scared. However, we don't have to resign ourselves to this sort of politics. We don't have to accept a government that insists upon pitting us against one another. We can and must do better.

In 2020, we face an emergency election of epic proportions. The next four years will undoubtedly impact the next 40, and the challenges we face are as daunting. More so than those who came before, our generation will pay the price for the inaction of our leaders. From climate change and health care to student debt and immigration, we'll be left footing the bill long after the policymakers of today leave office. Luckily, we hold the power. This year, young voters have the ability to decide the election and begin the process of restoring our

A Letter to U.S. College Students   153

democracy. To accomplish this, however, our generation must vote in record numbers.

As college students, we understand all too well the temptation to tune out our toxic politics. Far too often, it feels like those in Washington and capital cities across the country ignore our lived experiences and dismiss our very real concerns about the future. When activists and politicians urge us to mobilize and "make a difference," our participation can feel futile. After all, each of us has only one vote. How can we possibly change an entrenched system that has given us ballooning student loans, a degraded environment, and the prospect of a lower quality of life than our predecessors? The answer is not at all novel, for numerous generations of young people have shown us the way: we must vote. Not as individuals, but with one voice. We must vote like our futures are on the line. Vote to ensure our ability to give ourselves and our children prosperous, fulfilling lives. Vote to protect the rights of those who are like us and those who are not. We don't wish to be alarmist, and indeed there is reason for optimism in the face of these challenges, but we must make our voices heard.

At the time of this writing, our country and the world face the coronavirus pandemic. Americans across the nation are reckoning with the careless, negligent behavior of this president and his enablers as the stock market crashes and schools, small businesses, and public services are shut down. College students are being sent home, forced to complete our academic years remotely. At every turn, the Trump administration has sought to downplay the gravity of this crisis in service of the president's electoral fortunes. Americans in every region of our country are feeling the impact of this outbreak while congressional Republicans turn a blind eye to the danger at our doorstep. The extent of the economic and societal toll of this virus has yet to be fully realized, but never has the need for competent, compassionate leadership been greater.

It is not our intent to lecture about why *you* should care, but rather to share why *we* do. In doing so, we hope our stories will communicate what we believe is at stake in this election, and why we all must work to put an end to this poisonous period in our politics.

Immigration

Kara Johansen

Growing up in Dallas, Texas, the conversation about immigration was quite literally at my front door. Texas is one of five "majority-minority" states in the United States, primarily due to the large immigrant population from Mexico (albeit with many family lines residing in Texas since statehood) as well as South America.

While this may cause some insecurity among the former majority, it is also an opportunity to revel in greater diversity. Nonetheless, my neighborhood in Dallas is extremely conservative, and while I always found myself leaning toward the left, it was my personal connection to the realities of the immigrant experience that first sparked my passion for politics.

With both of my parents working full-time jobs, I was raised in large part by a nanny. Her name was Mira.[1] As a young child, little aware of power and privilege, I only thought of Mira braiding my hair before my preschool class, or her singing "You Are My Sunshine," and her listening to me talk about my day on the drive home from school. I still picture her laughing as I danced around the house, and her frowning as I talked about boys. I imagine the taste of her famous Mexican rice that I would always request for special occasions. Mira was truly a mother to me, and the love between us was an unbreakable bond.

It is that bond that forces me to think politically. As a child, I never understood her status as an undocumented person, even less that it may have been a defining fact of her life, opportunities, and choices in the United States. After all, in so many ways, she was another mother to me.

Now, however, I know that that experience deeply affected her. In Mexico, a land profoundly shaped by its unequal relationship with its powerful neighbor to the north, Mira lived in poverty. After the premature death of her mother, she suddenly became her family's primary caretaker. And, like many women on both sides of the border, she experienced physical abuse. After losing two children to malnutrition before she turned 17, Mira migrated to the United States. Defying the circumstances, she brought unimaginable compassion and grace that deeply touched the lives of everyone around her.

And then came the election of 2016.

For candidate Donald Trump, Mexicans were just "rapists and murderers." President Trump simply turned hateful rhetoric into brutal policy. Not only was it repugnant to my sense of human dignity, it simply flew in the face of the love that Mira exuded. Like so many undocumented people I came to know, Mira was an active member of her family, church, and community. She also taught me so much about what it meant to be a woman for others. She was a pillar in the lives of countless people, those who turned to her in moments of need. I count myself among those people.

Mira passed away in May of 2017, six months after Donald Trump was elected—six months during which fears of deportation weighed heavily on her mind. Although she had become a naturalized citizen by then, many of her friends and family were still at risk. They are fighting back and challenging the Trump administration. Nonetheless, 2020 is an emergency election because hate and fear remain operative. This is harmful because it aggravates xenophobia and identity politics, creating a dangerous sense of "us" versus "them." Justice for immigrants is not possible in a policy climate based on travel bans and zero-tolerance policies that tear families apart. As Americans, we must build on our sense of solidarity in this next election, recognizing the catastrophic impact of Trumpism on immigrant families and our own sense of self. For me, this means casting the vote that Mira is not here to cast.

Ways to Get Involved: National Immigrant Justice Center (www.immigrantjustice.org/how-help); National Immigration Law Center (www.nilc.org/#); ACLU Immigrant Rights (www.aclu.org/issues/immigrants-rights)

Health Care

Hannah LeBeau

It was Christmas Day in 2015. My stepmom was so weak she couldn't get out of bed. We opened presents with her, but she was so sick that even though she was physically present, she was barely there with us. It had been like this for a few days, so my parents decided that she needed to go to the emergency room. I stayed with my neighbor, waiting for my parents to get home. By the time Christmas dinner rolled around, they still hadn't returned. My stepmom was admitted to the hospital, where she would stay off and on for the next few months. Doctors repeatedly misdiagnosed her and prescribed medicine that never seemed to work. Each time she would grow sicker and sicker, and doctors would reassess and try something else. Weeks went by, and she was not improving, when luckily a doctor recognized her symptoms as those of a certain autoimmune disease. She was connected with a doctor in Boston who specializes in the disease, and she slowly was able to recover. However, even after she left the hospital, she was left with the burden of monthly treatments and daily medications in order to prevent further hospitalization.

My stepmom's health struggle underscored the shortcomings of the American health care system. My family is privileged because we have health care that covered my stepmom both during her hospitalization and afterward. But what about those who don't? Getting sick is expensive, and chronic conditions even more so. Will people who are uninsured have to suffer or die as a consequence for being unable to afford the care they both need and deserve? The reality is, yes, they will. Estimates vary, but most research indicates that tens of thousands die each year in the United States as a result of being uninsured.

Going into this election in 2020, the contrast between our two parties couldn't be clearer. Democrats are fighting to ensure that health care is treated by our government as an inalienable human right, while the current administration seeks to repeal the Affordable Care Act and do away with basic benefits that increase access to quality, affordable health care.

Examples of basic benefits provided by Obamacare include the following:

- You are able to stay on your parent's insurance until you are 26 years old
- You cannot be denied insurance for having a pre-existing condition
- Your insurance cannot drop you because you get sick
- There is no limit to the amount of care you can receive in a year

If the Affordable Care Act is repealed, Americans of all backgrounds will feel the impacts. The Trump administration's crusade to end his predecessor's landmark accomplishment will make access to health care more difficult for families across the United States. We need affordable, quality health care that is accessible at all times, and people shouldn't be penalized for seeking treatment when sick. Even if you're completely healthy and don't need to worry about health care, you never know when your life could turn upside down and you could face a serious illness like my stepmom did. My family's story is far from unique. We can't afford four more years of full-frontal assault on Americans' right to affordable health care. In 2020, we must vote for our care, which has become a top priority in the era of the coronavirus.

Ways to Get Involved: Universal Health Care Action Network (https://uhcan.org/); National Coalition on Health Care (https://nchc.org/); Healthcare NOW! (www.healthcare-now.org/action-center/)

Environment

Conor Hicks

I was born and raised in Central Oregon's High Desert, situated alongside the Deschutes National Forest. The arid climate in which I grew up is extremely vulnerable to the threat of wildfires. My childhood summers became synonymous with smoke-filled skies and poor air quality, putting my community's health at risk. Faced with heavy smoke, children and seniors alike are forced to stay indoors for the sake of their wellbeing. Each fire season, countless homes are threatened and livelihoods placed in jeopardy.

It's impossible to discuss wildfires without recognizing the exacerbating effect of climate change. As the climate crisis has worsened, fire season has lengthened, and the threat to people in the West has only increased. Summers are hotter and drier, and precipitation rates have declined in regions like mine, creating more fuel for the flames.

As communities across the West have watched forest fires become more frequent and even more dangerous due to the climate crisis, our government under President Donald Trump has abdicated its duty to protect our environment. Since taking office, the president and his allies in the energy industry have gutted the Environmental Protection Agency and rolled back countless regulations designed to protect our country's natural beauty and address the impacts of climate change. They've consistently prioritized short-term profits over the long-term prosperity of our generation, and have sold out our children's future in the name of a quick buck.

While it isn't too late to solve the many challenges the climate crisis poses, we're running out of time. Just as we do, our planet faces an emergency election in 2020. Extending the Trump agenda opens the door to four more years of inaction on our most pressing environmental issues. Four more years of regressive climate policies that undermine our generation's quality of life. Our future is inextricably linked to the health of our environment, and we can't afford to wait any longer to combat this crisis. It's time to put our planet first at the ballot box.

Conner Coles

On a clear summer morning, I was awoken from my sleep in fear as the unthinkable began to occur. In my hometown of Edmond, Oklahoma, an earthquake shook my entire neighborhood. The first rumblings were enough to put the members of my household on edge, and the aftershocks elicited confusion and bewilderment. In the following months, what began first as an anomaly became a common occurrence. The earthquakes increased in regularity and strength. In Pawnee, Oklahoma, in September of 2016, a 5.8 magnitude tremor became the highest ever recorded in our state's history. In 2010, Oklahoma had 41 observed earthquakes. By 2015, that number was 900. This discrepancy cannot not be explained by natural phenomena. The cause was undoubtedly anthropogenic and the result of a deliberate set of policy decisions.

The cause of the increase in earthquakes in Oklahoma and in many other states is the increased use of fracking as a means for oil and natural gas extraction. Fracking is a process in which a combination of water, sand, and chemicals are injected into rock at high pressure to release oil and gas from the shale. The practice has dramatically increased in popularity, with the number of wells increasing from 23,000 in 2000 to 300,000 in 2015. The Trump administration appointed as its first EPA director the former Oklahoma Attorney General Scott Pruitt. Under the leadership of Pruitt and Trump, regulations on drilling new wells have been slashed, and federal lands open to fracking have been tripled to 12.8 million acres.

Fracking and the earthquakes it triggers have become all too common in my state and many others. They are normalized so that outrage is no longer elicited. This is something which is emblematic of Trumpism. What once caused shock and condemnation has become one item among a long list of scandals and crimes. We must treat 2020 as an emergency election to prevent the ideology that prioritizes profit over the environment and disregards the safety of the majority of Americans for the benefit and expedience of a few from irreversibly taking hold.

Ways to Get Involved: Sierra Club (www.sierraclub.org/take-action); League of Conservation Voters (www.lcv.org/get-involved/); Sunrise Movement (www.sunrisemovement.org/join); Zero Hour (http://thisiszerohour.org/donate/)

Student Debt

Sophie Carter and Julianna Carbone

As a college student, there is nothing that makes our heart skip a beat quite like receiving an email notification from the financial aid office. There is always something going wrong in the vast bureaucracy of

A Letter to U.S. College Students 159

student loans and scholarships, with misunderstandings, lost documents, confusion, stress, and unclear deadlines looming as we wait for confirmation on whether our application has been approved. The uncertainty can be exhausting. Something as simple as a misplaced tax return from two years ago can make the difference between being able to continue going to school as scheduled and needing to scramble to make a different plan.

Over the decades, the cost of a college education has been steadily increasing, and it is only going to continue to rise. The average cost of an in-state, public school tuition in 2020 is $25,000, and many private colleges are creeping up in price, sometimes nearing as much as $80,000 a year. Even with aid from the federal government, the cost of going to college is unaffordable for many low-income and middle-class families, and many students in our generation are faced with a difficult choice between not going to college at all and being in debt for decades.

This choice is severely restricted by the context of our time. At the same time that the sticker price of a college education skyrockets, so does the necessity of a college degree. Eleven out of the top 15 fastest-growing professions in the United States require at least a bachelor's degree. There is a narrowing path to socioeconomic mobility, and it increasingly involves going to college. In order to have a chance at a better future for ourselves, we have to take on a massive investment for ourselves—in the form of thousands of dollars in debt, with high interest rates accumulating over time.

This is an emergency election for college students like us who are struggling with student debt and the cost of college. Approximately 70% of students end up taking out loans, and the average student finishes college with roughly $37,000 in loans, making the collective student loan debt in America upward of $1.5 trillion. Sure, there are standard payment plans in play, but depending on degrees, it can be difficult to fit the mold of some of these plans. Society tells us that if we go to college, we will get a better job, make more money, and therefore have a better life, thus rationalizing the burden of a loan. However, even after graduating, some entry-level salaries are not enough to keep up with the 10-year payment plan, yet, for every year that 10-year period increases, so does the interest on the loan, and in turn, the profit of our federal government.

On small-scale, local levels, efforts are being made to combat the debt program. In Rhode Island, Governor Gina Raimondo made community college tuition-free through an income-share agreement, meaning that depending on degree and post-grad job, a student will be required to pay a percentage of their income for a fixed number of years after graduation. Recently, Purdue University, headed by former Indiana Governor Mitch Daniels, has begun to do the same with a small percentage of their student body through the Back a Boiler Program. This income-share agreement and other efforts to create "free college" in America like in Tennessee, Oregon, and New York may not be the answer, but it is important that, at the federal level, this burden of student debt that so many Americans face is prioritized and dealt with on a far greater scale than initiated by policymakers as the coronavirus exploded. And the first step to this solution is our student vote in 2020.

Ways to Get Involved: Student Debt Crisis Organization (www.studentdebtcrisis.org); Rolling Jubilee (www.rollingjubilee.org); Higher Ed, Not Debt (www.higherednotdebt.org)

LGBTQ+ Rights

Morgan Jemtrud

In my experience, there was no "lightbulb" moment when I realized I liked women in a way that I had never liked men. It was a sort of series of events—not having a boy-crazy phase like my sister and cousin, fixating on female characters in books and movies while ignoring their male counterparts, and never considering the men around me to be attractive in a way that made me want to be with them, to name a few—that led me gently to the word "lesbian." In theory, it could have been the easiest coming-out experience in the world. Naturally, that didn't happen.

I'm from the American South, a region that has never been known for its love of the LGBTQ community, a reality that kept me quiet for years. And from my point of view, deep within the closet, I watched in horror in 2016 as Donald Trump was elected. The effects were immediate in my Kentucky high school, as the amount of hate speech and physical attacks against minorities skyrocketed. Walking through the hallways, I was choked by my own identity while I listened to my peers—supported by the rhetoric of the president and vice president of the United States—dehumanize me and everyone who shared my identity.

Maybe some of you reading this felt the same way then, and you feel the same way now—that soul-tearing pain of having your identity twisted into something repulsive and inhuman. If you haven't,

A Letter to U.S. College Students 161

I can assure you that it hurts in a way that words fail to capture. It is imperative that we treat all Americans as equal, and it is imperative that we treat all Americans with dignity. And so I, like the rest of my peers, am begging you—the voices of America's future—to vote for a better future for us all.

Ways to Get Involved: Human Rights Campaign (www.hrc.org/support); Victory Fund (https://victoryfund.org/take-action/); Lambda Legal (https://lambdalegal.org/take-action); The Trevor Project (www.thetrevorproject.org/get-involved/); It Gets Better Project (https://itgetsbetter.org/)

Conclusion

The challenges that we all must face are unprecedented in human history. Climate change is an existential threat to every species on the planet, and it cannot be solved by one nation alone. Even the challenges that face the United States—providing affordable health care to all, reducing inequality and raising wages, ending the epidemic of gun violence, reducing the bloated military budget and stopping endless wars, among many others—will require a generational response. The task ahead is too large to be faced solely by one political party, one ideology, or within a certain region of the United States or the world. We all must work together. Our generation has the least ties to the past and the biggest stake in the future, and we cannot afford to stay on the sidelines. We must not let the decisions that are determining the course of our lives be made without our imprint. For far too long we have trusted and deferred to other generations, but no more.

The power is in our hands, and we must not feel apathy or bewilderment regarding the task before us. Every great movement begins with a single act of courage and conviction that inspires others to action. Be it protesting, canvassing, calling on behalf of a candidate or campaign, or the simple act of voting, we all must do our part. The election of 2016 demonstrated the threat of deferring our responsibility, while the election of 2018 showcased our power to change our destiny. No outcome in society is ever set in stone. For too long, our generation has resigned itself to a future dictated by those who came before us. No more. The 2020 election is the most important election of our lifetimes, and must be treated as an emergency. The gravity of this moment demands that we commit ourselves to the restoration of the promise of America and the free world.

We have the power to create a world that reflects our values. The danger we face from inaction is not simply that progressive policies will not be passed. The peril is in what the ruling agenda represents: distortion, division, and prejudice. If these values are allowed to triumph here and be replicated elsewhere, it will be impossible for our country and the nations of the world to move forward. The values of acceptance, truth, and unity must win the day. The only way to achieve this victory is through our collective participation at the ballot box. Martin Luther King, Jr., famously said, "The moral arc of the universe is long, but it bends toward justice." It must be the undertaking of students across America to be the spark that again bends the arc. Throughout modern history it has been students and young people on the frontlines of creating change, from the civil rights movement to the Women's March. We must take up the mantle of history and the legacy of previous generations of young activists, and live up to the challenges of our time. The task before us is far from easy. We face an onslaught of dark money and special interests hellbent on prolonging the agenda dominating the White House. They know that if we as young voters stay home, they'll win. They're counting on us tuning out the vitriol and corruption espoused by the administration each and every day. In November, we need to prove them wrong.

So today we're asking you to make a plan. Update your voter registration. Research the positions of candidates at every level of government and decide whom to support. Locate your polling place and mark election day (**November 3, 2020**) on your calendar. Above all, get engaged with the issues you care about and join the fight to retake our democracy. The organizations we've suggested are just a few among countless more dedicated to this endeavor. We've got a lot of work to do, but together we can create a brighter future for all of us. Let's go.

Your Fellow Students,

Conor L. Hicks (Redmond, OR)
Conner Coles (Edmond, OK)
Julianna Carbone (Boca Raton, FL)
Morgan Jemtrud (Crestwood, KY)
Sophia Carter (Warwick, RI)
Audrey Vas (Corte Madera, CA)
Hannah LeBeau (West Palm Beach, FL)
Kara Johansen (Highland Park, TX)
John Gehman (Royersford, PA)

Note

1. Out of respect for Mira and her family, I have provided her with a pseudonym.

Contributors

Editors

Charles Derber is Professor of Sociology at Boston College and a noted public intellectual. Professor Derber has written 23 books, including several best-sellers reviewed in the *New York Times*, the *Washington Post*, the *Boston Globe*, and other leading media. His most recent books include *Welcome to the Revolution*, *Moving Beyond Fear*, and *Glorious Causes*. He is a co-editor of the Routledge book series Universalizing Resistance, and is a life-long activist for peace and justice.

Suren Moodliar is editor of the journal *Socialism and Democracy* and coordinator of encuentro5, a movement-building space in downtown Boston. He is a co-author of *A People's Guide to Greater Boston* (UC Press, 2020).

Matt Nelson is Executive Director of Presente.org—the nation's largest online Latinx organizing group, advancing social justice with technology, media, and culture. Matt also served as the organizing director at ColorOfChange.org and has co-founded several cooperative enterprises in multiple Midwestern cities. He was recently featured in the first major book on the Ferguson Uprising, *Ferguson Is America: Roots of Rebellion*. He is finishing a new book on how Latinx organizing and cultural power are reshaping US politics (Routledge, 2020).

Contributors

Katherine Adam is a vice president at the communications firm Denterlein.

Contributors

Aimee Allison is the founder of She the People.

Karthik Balasubramanian is Professor of Information Systems & Supply Chain Management at Howard University.

Mandela Barnes is the Lieutenant-Governor of Wisconsin.

Nikki Fortunato Bas is an Oakland City Councilor.

Medea Benjamin is a co-founder of Code Pink.

LaTosha Brown and **Cliff Albright** are founders of the Black Voters Matter Fund.

Noam Chomsky is Emeritus Institute Professor Institute Professor at the Massachusetts Institute of Technology and Laureate professor in the Department of Linguistics at the University of Arizona.

Debra Cleaver is the founder and CEO of Turnout2020.

Jennifer Epps-Addison is the Network President and Co-Executive Director of the Center for Popular Democracy.

Dana R. Fisher is a sociologist based at the University of Maryland.

Helen Gym is a Philadelphia City Councilor.

Ian Haney López is Professor of Public Law at the University of California, Berkeley.

Steve Israel, U.S. Congressman 2001–2017, directs the nonpartisan Institute of Politics and Global Affairs at Cornell University.

Saru Jayaraman is a co-founder of the Restaurant Opportunities Centers United.

Deborah Klebansky and **Kira Moodliar** are student activists at McGill University.

Maria Teresa Kumar is President of Voto Latino.

Winona LaDuke is Executive Director of Honor the Earth.

Annie Leonard is Executive Director of Greenpeace US.

Ben Manski is President of the Liberty Tree Foundation for the Democratic Revolution.

Bill McKibben is the founder of 350.org.

Jeff Merkley represents Oregon in the U.S. Senate.

Contributors 165

Stephanie Nakajima is Director of Communications at Healthcare NOW!

Wilnelia Rivera is President of Rivera Consulting, Inc.

Anat Shenker-Osorio is the principal and founder of ASO Communications.

Nancy Treviño is the Presente.org's Senior Campaign Manager.

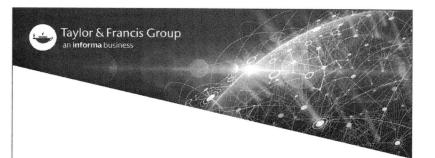

Taylor & Francis eBooks

www.taylorfrancis.com

A single destination for eBooks from Taylor & Francis with increased functionality and an improved user experience to meet the needs of our customers.

90,000+ eBooks of award-winning academic content in Humanities, Social Science, Science, Technology, Engineering, and Medical written by a global network of editors and authors.

TAYLOR & FRANCIS EBOOKS OFFERS:

- A streamlined experience for our library customers
- A single point of discovery for all of our eBook content
- Improved search and discovery of content at both book and chapter level

REQUEST A FREE TRIAL
support@taylorfrancis.com